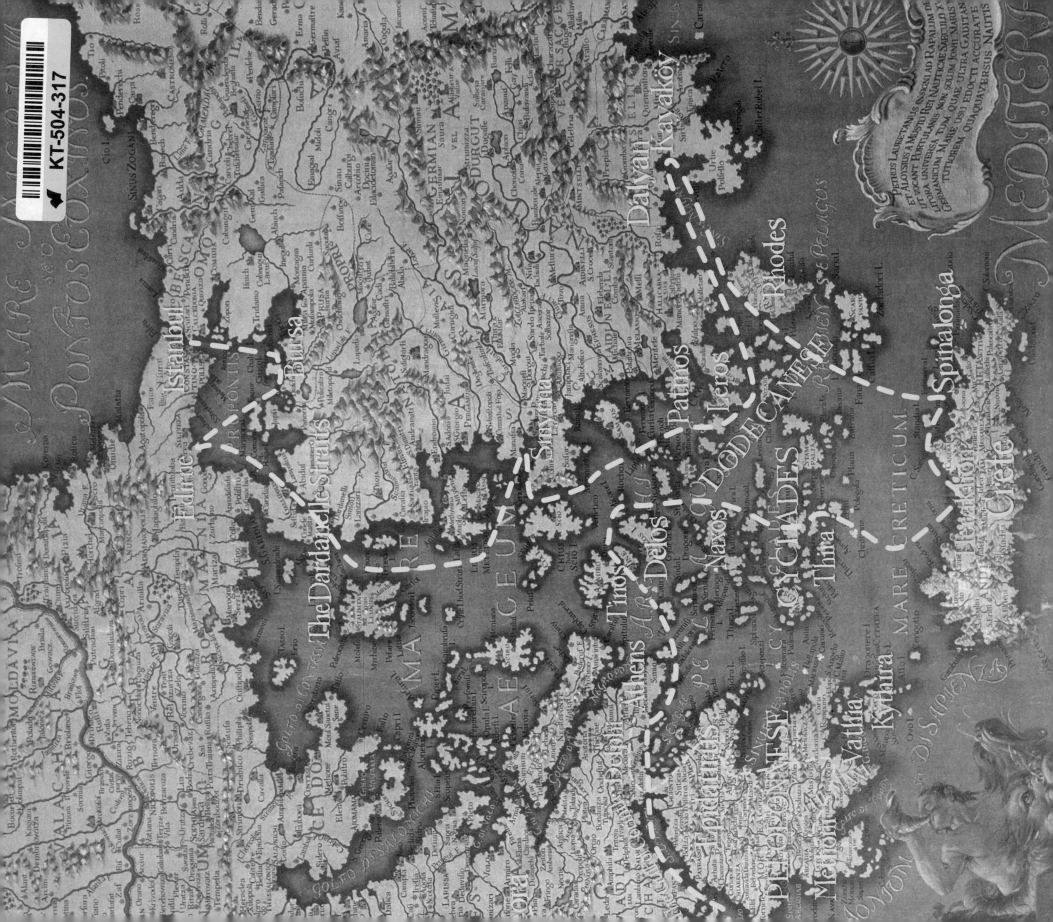

FRANCESCO'S
MEDITERRANEAN VOYAGE

FRANCESCO'S MEDITERRANEAN VOYAGE

FRANCESCO DA MOSTO

PHOTOGRAPHS BY JOHN PARKER

BBC
BOOKS

CONTENTS

INTRODUCTION

AMONG MY EARLIEST childhood memories, from even before I could read, I recall climbing up the staircase at home where, on the landing, there had always been a marble bust of a gentleman with long hair. I was told that he was an ancestor, a navigator and an explorer who'd lived long before us: Alvise da Mosto. Since then, I have tended to keep my hair long and have dreamed of exploring the world.

My hair, still long, may now have turned grey but the desire to sail the seas is as strong as ever. Therefore it was a dream come true when the BBC asked me to travel from Venice to Istanbul (formerly Constantinople) in a sailing boat following the Venetian routes to the Levant. This evocative word literally means 'east', coming from the French *lever* (lift), which refers to the point of sunrise; in the fifteenth century, however, it was also used in the sense of 'Mediterranean lands east of Venetia'.

Even though I now had a family – small children and a wife whom I knew I would miss and that they would miss me – the desire to put myself to the test and get level with my ancestors by exploring some new places was too great to resist. This would be a different experience: retracing the steps of my forebears to the East, through the Mediterranean. Five centuries of history separate Alvise da Mosto, twenty years old and an explorer of necessity, and me, his descendant, dreamer by chance and double his age.

Alvise showed me the route that the navigators followed in the fifteenth century, when navigation depended on working out latitude from the stars and longitude from the parchment maps of earlier explorers, guided by his acclaimed vade mecum (handbook), the *Portolano del Mediterraneo*. Sailing aboard the *Black Swan*, an 1899 yawl exemplary of England's finest boat-

ABOVE The Rialto Bridge spans the Grand Canal, an emblem of Venice's trading tradition.

BELOW Istanbul at nightfall, as seen from the Golden Horn.

building traditions, I followed in his wake and discovered what remains of the glories of *La Serenissima*, Venetian traditions and their influences on art, architecture and culture.

Along the way, touching the coasts of the Adriatic, Ionian and Aegean seas, I also dug deeper into the remoter past of the region. These are the waters that Aeneas and Odysseus sailed; the islands that, in ancient legend, were home to sirens, Cyclops and lotus-eaters; the cities, states and kingdoms where governments (oligarchies and democracies) were first formed, and where the great philosophers Plato and Aristotle first articulated the human condition.

Passing through the Aegean, it is sobering to think that in Athens and the city-states and islands surrounding it, 3,000 years ago the sun of Western civilization rose. Seeing these places – not just the museums and treasures, but also the sky and earth – it is possible to understand how everything we have today in art, philosophy, politics and science began there, one way or another. And at the heart of this civilization was not land, but sea, the Mediterranean, and the trading ships and warring vessels that traversed its waters also spread ideas and technologies.

But it is impossible to suppress the reality of today – customs and costumes, the changes of mentality, technology, culture, wealth, attitudes to God, history and its events. And in the part of the Adriatic bordering the Balkans, I saw where and how different populations and religions have clashed recently – but also where much has already been done to heal the situation.

My journey ended sailing into the Golden Horn in Istanbul. With its long bridges and shorelines, vast mosques and palaces, this city was the political epicentre of the Ottoman Empire from the fifteenth to the twentieth century. If Alvise set off in the prime of his youth, I reached Istanbul in the years of my maturity, at about the same age as the Venetian artist Gentile Bellini when he was despatched as a kind of cultural ambassador to the court of the Sultan, Mehmet II, to rekindle relations with the Turks. My voyage may not have had the same relevance or importance as Bellini's, who, through art, managed to bring two worlds and religions – East and West, Christianity and Islam – closer together. However, the two of us shared a common point of origin, Venice, as well as the journey between two continents, Europe and Asia, with a myriad of islands and other realities in between.

THE *PORTOLANO* ATTRIBUTED TO ALVISE DA MOSTO

According to Francesco Sansovino's *Venezia città nobilissima e singolare*, published in 1663, Alvise da Mosto died in 1477. The same book describes him as, 'a highly diligent patrician, explorer of the seas; at the age of 22 he travelled as far as the port of Scussa in lower Ethiopia; Colombus was moved by his example and discovered the New World; he wrote a book entitled the *Portolano*, but without his name.' The manuscript is preserved in the Museo Correr and the first version of the *Portolano*, printed in Venice by Bernardino Rizo on 6 December 1490, begins like this: 'This is a necessary work for all navigators who go to different parts of the world, all can learn from it to recognize landfalls, anchorings, bays, valleys, ports, water-flows and tides'. It ends with these words:

So finishes the book called Portolano composed by a Venetian gentleman who has seen all the places described here, which are very useful for all navigators who want to navigate in safety in their ships to the various parts of the world.

This *Portolano* was not initially attributed to anyone; one of the various editions bore a letter from the publisher to the Procurator of St Mark:

This Portolano having come into my hands and being considered by knowledgeable people the most complete that could be desired in these matters, I felt the wish to

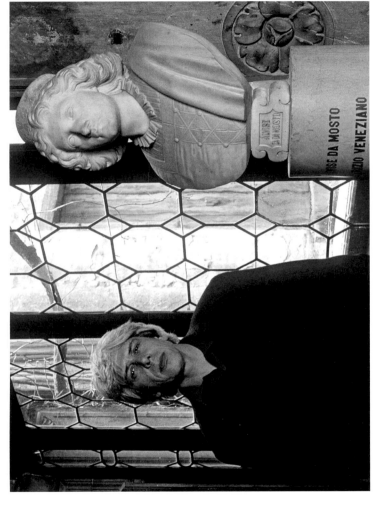

Alvise and me, just after I'd told him that this time he'd have to stay at home!

bring it to public notice, so that it might be of advantage to anyone who has to ply the salt waves of the sea of Venice and the Mediterranean where the sun sets and rises; without any doubt in the safe company of this book anyone might make a voyage. As this book voyages without the name of its author I judged it best to illuminate it with the ray of your singular virtue… And in such splendour of Venetian glory my devotion places it in the light of your glory.

I admire Alvise's modesty-cum-absent-mindedness; his presence is still greatly felt in my family. Every day I pass his statue outside my studio and I hear him whisper: 'So when are you going to put your wings on and fly?' He started his voyages aged 14, working on the ships of the Contarini family, following the trade routes to

Flanders. He then left Venice aged 19 when he was given the opportunity by the Portuguese Infante, Henry the Navigator, to captain a trading-ship to West Africa.

Alvise probably went to Portugal because his father was in trouble with the Venetian authorities, which limited his prospects in Venice. Family circumstances today are decidedly uncompli-cated by comparison – I even feel certain obligations to stay here to try to contribute to a genuine revitalization of the city, its traditions

and its heritage, building upon my family background. But on the other hand, being reminded of intrepid ancestors is an inspiration, teasing me and challenging me to explore the world more widely.

I didn't just set out on this journey with a photograph of Alvise's statue, but with his writings too. My good friend Giuseppe happened to have a 1737 reprint of *Consolato del Mare* by Francesco Piacentini containing the *Portolano* as well as numerous navigation laws of the Serene Republic. Without even asking, Giuseppe offered me the volume, saying, 'its name is Jack because it must come back.'

With pragmatic and lucid details, Alvise tells you all the special shapes and signs by which you can recognize any point of the coast at a glance, the best places of access, the rocks and shallows, the depth of the water, the trade centres and the most important goods to be found there. It describes all the landing places along the coasts, gives directions on how to reach them and the distances between them.

1

STARTING OUT

The *Bacino di San Marco*, looking towards San Giorgio, where the galleons would moor prior to departure.

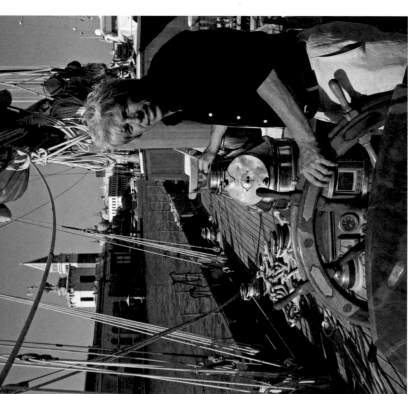

VENICE

M Y CITY IS BEAUTIFUL, but it is falling apart and we Venetians are becoming an endangered species. There are only 65,000 of us left among the 15 million visitors a year: tourism has taken over our economy and many who come here no longer even think of the Venice they find today as a living, breathing entity. But once, this island city was the centre of a vast and mighty empire with literally millions of citizens. Its name suggested much more than just weekend breaks and souvenirs – it meant trade, power and war: Venice, Queen of the Adriatic, City of Water, Most Serene Republic.

I grew up surrounded by reminders of who my ancestors were, including some impressive characters like Antonio da Mosto, admiral of the Venetian navy, or Nicolò da Mosto, army paymaster (before he headed out to sea on a military expedition). Now the city is clearly humbled and we Venetians have mostly lost our direction; I missed Venice's golden age by about three centuries, but instead of dwelling in the past, or brooding over the vacuousness of the town today, I am setting sail in search of Venice's Mediterranean empire.

According to Casanova, 'a Venetian who has never visited our eastern territories is like a cat who has never caught a mouse.' Well, I am a Venetian, so this is a journey I simply must make, and an opportunity to make it in the style offered by the *Black Swan* does not come along every day. The *Black Swan* was built in 1899 and has since been through numerous incarnations, up to her most recent modernization just a few years ago. It is reputedly one of the largest and oldest classic sailing yachts in the world, and is also extremely comfortable with five wood-panelled cabins, an air-conditioning system, hot water on demand and even a room-to-room intercom system. She has unrelenting charisma and majestic style.

OPPOSITE A Venetian canal: roads of water that were the easiest way for us Venetians to move around at home as well as in the Mediterranean.

ABOVE Finally aboard the boat, I couldn't wait to take the helm.

13

secure (at least from invaders). While most of Europe was lost in the Dark Ages, we Venetians consolidated our power. Sustained initially by the wealth of fish in the surrounding waters and salt production, we foraged on nearby shores for supplies and those shores gradually moved further and further afield. The essential supplies grew to become trading goods and soon we were no longer underdogs, but masters.

Every year for the last thousand years we have celebrated the union of Venice and the Mediterranean Sea, and the notorious wealth this brought, by tossing a wedding ring into the lagoon. But in Venice today water is viewed as the city's enemy; it makes modern life taxing, the buildings are in ruins and the canal water creeps up the walls and causes bricks to crumble. Everything is overshadowed by the risks of flooding. We seem to have forgotten what it was that made Venice great and politicians are increasingly oriented towards transforming the unique *città d'acqua* into just a suburb of the more recent and banal urbanization on the mainland.

It is the water of the lagoon that connects Venice to Istanbul and Athens, to Alexandria and Genoa. Far more than just a liquid, it's the source of power and civilization itself. My most accomplished ancestor Alvise da Mosto, who discovered the Cape Verde Islands in the mid-fifteenth century when the world was pictured 'upside down' (with the south at the top and the north at the bottom), was a great navigator of the Mediterranean as well. Following his *Portolano*, or logbook, I'm going to make my way to Istanbul from Venice, as he did:

Starting from Venice, going eastwards to Constantinople and to Alexandria and the whole of Syria, seeking the islands of the sea, landfalls, ports, vales and bays. Venice is a large city in the sea, 3 to 4 miles from the land to the south and about one to the west.

ALVISE DA MOSTO, *PORTOLANO*, 1490

THE SEAT OF POWER

All Venice's power emanated from the Palazzo Ducale, the home of the Doge, his civil servants, the law courts and the prisons. The *Sala dello Scudo* is a room decorated with immense maps that show not only the lands that belonged to the Venetian Republic (including much of the northern mainland of the Italian peninsula, the coast of Dalmatia, the Greek islands and even, for one brief moment, Constantinople itself) but also the known world in the shape of the three continents: Europe, Asia and Africa.

OPPOSITE The Doge's Palace.

ABOVE Low tide in the lagoon reveals the mudflats amid the open waters.

BLACK SWAN LOG

So tonight is going to be a special one, with all the family, and Venice. My youngest son Pierangelo has been looking forward to this occasion for months. He is a pyromaniac and tonight is the Festa del Redentore (Redeemer), when we celebrate the city's deliverance from the Great Plague 500 years ago, with a fantastic fireworks display. There were some drawbacks to being a large trading empire: if a disease broke out anywhere in the world, we were bound to get it eventually. The plague of 1575 killed over a quarter of the population.

ABOVE A map from the *Sala dello Scudo* (Shield Room) of the Doge's Palace, drawn up by the cosmographer Francesco Grisellini in the late eighteenth century, after paintings by G. B. Ramusio. He, in turn, had followed the indications of Alvise and another patrician, Pietro Loredan – see the Latin inscription translated opposite.

RIGHT Globes showing the world after the discovery of America.

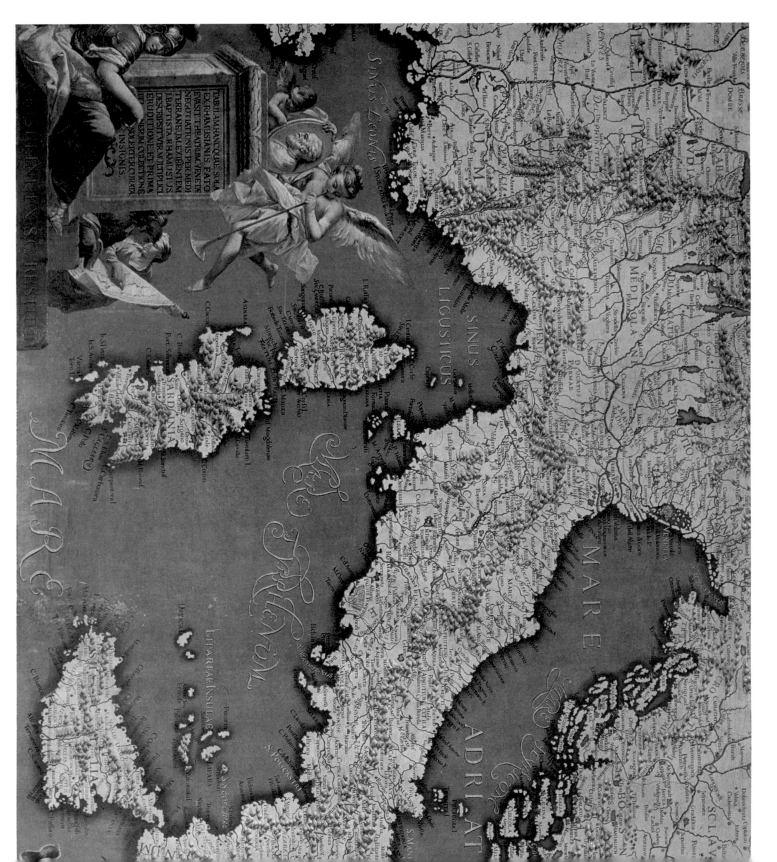

PIETRO LOREDAN, FAMOUS FOR HIS GREAT VICTORY OVER THE GENOESE NEAR RAPALLO,
AND ALVISE DA MOSTO, FAMOUS FOR THE ART OF SAILING IN THE FIFTEENTH CENTURY,
COMPOSED WITH SKILL THE *PORTOLANI* – AS THEY ARE KNOWN – FROM THEIR EXPERIENCE.
THEY ACCURATELY DESCRIBED NOT ONLY THE SHORES OF THE IONIAN AND THE AEGEAN
SEA, BUT ALSO ALL THE COASTS THAT RUN FROM BEYOND THE STRAITS OF GIBRALTAR TO
THE NORTH SEA. WITH THIS MANUAL THEY MADE THE WAY SAFER FOR SAILORS.

BLACK SWAN LOG

The Redentore is one of the oldest and most popular festivals in Venice, and it is celebrated at the church of the same name, another of Palladio's sacred masterpieces, on the third Sunday of July. A ritual that has been repeated for over 400 years, the city is joined to the island of the Giudecca by a floating bridge, and on the eve of the religious celebrations everyone gathers in and around the lagoon area directly in front of St Mark's, first to eat, then to enjoy the fireworks at midnight. Venetians are the real protagonists for once; their boats are decorated with colourful festoons, lanterns and vine leaves, and the houses, balconies and quaysides are illuminated with coloured lights. We weave our way through the maze of crafts to get nearer where the fireworks are set off. Up close, the spectacle is thrilling: when the rockets burst, they shower us with light and the bangs reverberate in our chests; then down come the sparks, cascading around us.

ABOVE The church of *Il Redentore* seen across the *Bacino* with Punta della Dogana in the foreground. OPPOSITE Entrance to the Arsenale with a collection of marble lions taken from Athens, Corfu and Delos.

These paintings celebrate Venetian dominion over the waves. The sea is shown offering up its treasures to Venice, depicted as a beautiful woman; countless canvases record her great victories at sea, like the huge painting by Paolo Veronese, which shows the Doge offering thanks after defeating the Turks at Lepanto in 1571. In the north of the city the buildings of the Arsenale (the city's docklands) remain. It was reputedly the busiest place in Europe with 300 shipping companies employing 16,000 people, loading and unloading, making and equipping ships. Famously capable of assembling a ship in a day, when King Henry III of France visited the city, an entire galley was built in the same time as the banquet in his honour! By the mid-fifteenth century they had already implemented the assembly-line system here; specific tasks were compartmentalized, quality checks were carried out on all raw materials and the methods of production were standardized – not far from the concepts adopted in factories today.

The Turks were the other great Mediterranean power – and the sworn enemies of Venice. The story of Marcantonio Bragadin, one of the most famous Venetian combatants, is an example of one of the many times when Venice didn't come out on top. Starting in the mid-1500s, Bragadin had a distinguished naval career including important military assignments on Venetian galleons; then, in 1569, he was elected governor of the Kingdom of Cyprus he went straight to Famagusta to prepare for an inevitable clash with the Ottoman fleet. He put up a

VENETIAN MEDITERRANEAN NAVIGATION THROUGH THE AGES

Over the centuries Venetians have not confined themselves to short-haul sailing, but have also embarked on long-haul journeys, venturing out around the Mediterranean and into the Atlantic to the countries of Northern Europe.

Short-haul commercial traffic was generally confined to the Upper Adriatic and internal waters, with only brief excursions into the open sea. It was conducted using craft with round prows and flat bottoms, which were suited to sailing in shallow coastal waters and lagoons. These vessels, which transported wine, grain, salt, stones and timber, were generally propelled by oar, although they also had sails.

The unpredictability of the Mediterranean led the English to name it the 'sea of seas'. Ships in the Adriatic and in the Aegean have always had to cope with very variable meteorological conditions, ranging from long periods of complete calm to storms and strong winds known as the Bora, Scirocco, Mistral and Meltemi. Indeed, the second part of our journey to Istanbul was conditioned by the Meltemi, which blows throughout August and September. This added to the navigational challenges of the Aegean, which, with its thousands of islands and rocks and shallow ports, is difficult at the best of times, but becomes almost impossible in bad weather.

Long-haul sailing ships were stocky in shape, being roughly three times as long as they were broad, with two decks, one forecastle, one quarterdeck and a fighting top. They were governed with two side-rudders, which were sometimes linked to a central bar. They used no oars and had two or three masts leaning towards the prow with lateen sails. However, as they couldn't sail against the wind at an angle of less than 80 to 85 degrees (with respect to the provenance of the wind) they sailed with the wind to the side, and, on account of the weight of the ship, with notable leeway. For their size they were excellent for cargo, with a weight limit that often exceeded 500 tons.

Other craft that sailed the same waters were the so-called round ships, used for transporting animals and goods, which were loaded through large hatches in the stern. They were adopted by Venice during the Fourth Crusade, when Doge Enrico Dandolo attacked Constantinople – on this occasion they were used to transport almost 5,000 horses and thousands of infantry troops, plus provisions for the duration of the whole expedition.

Meanwhile in northern Europe a new kind of round ship – the *cocca* or cog – had been developed, which arrived in the Mediterranean around the beginning of the fourteenth century, possibly with the corsairs. These were also stocky boats, with a square stern and central helm. The large mainmast had a square sail (and sometimes also a mizzen-mast with a lateen sail). The square sail was easier to manoeuvre than a lateen sail and required less manpower – thus, the crew could be halved in size, making it possible to embark more soldiers, cannons and goods.

My ancestor Alvise, who began sailing in the Atlantic Ocean in the mid-fifteenth century, used yet another kind of vessel, the *caravella*, or caravel, as noted in his log: 'As I was still at Cape St Vincent, the Infante Henry showed that he was very pleased and welcomed me heartily: and then many many days later he equipped a new caravel for me of about 90 tuns [about 45 tons in today's weights or half as big as the *Black Swan*].' These were light, swift ships of low tonnage, with three masts and lateen sails but also the square cog of the round, long and narrow ships. During my journey, I was also reminded of the *Nave Mosta*, a 302-ton caravel owned by brothers Francesco and Bortolomio da Mosto. In its day it was one of the four largest ships in Venice, able to carry 110 men, 45 of them sailors. In 1504, while on its way from Cyprus to Corfu with a cargo of salt, the anchor and hawser were lost and the shrouds damaged. Once back at the Arsenale in Venice it was granted the loan of a hawser with a leaded 12-carat chain, and was then requisitioned by the *Serenissima* government for the war against the Turks, at a rent of 300 ducats. Three years later, Francesco da Mosto, the captain of the ship, died in combat. The ship was eventually seized by the Turks (together with a rich cargo of Malmsey wine belonging to various noblemen) and pressed into the Turkish fleet.

A model of a sixteenth-century Venetian galley at the Naval Museum.

The unmistakable colours of Venice are the combined result of a special light and the reflections of the sky in the water.

brave and unequal fight for many months, but was eventually captured. The Turks cut his ears off and flayed him alive. His skin was stuffed with straw and then mounted on a cow and paraded through the streets, before being sent back to Venice on the front of a ship.

Overall, the Venetians managed to resist the Ottoman advances in the Mediterranean for centuries, until the Republic's might began to disintegrate. Perhaps Venice had become too avaricious, her people wallowing in legendary decadence – either way the great powers, not least the Ottomans, took advantage of these weaknesses, while other nations and states gained an increased share of the world trading that previously had been dominated by the Venetians.

The winged lion, symbol of Venice, represents St Mark the Evangelist, her patron saint.

The lion of Venice lost its strength, becoming just a statue, a piece of stone dotted around the Mediterranean in memory of the depth and breadth of the *Serenissima*. And the city dwindled into a mere playground for Europe's aristocracy, famous only for its carnivals, casinos and courtesans, all embodied in the most notorious 'C' of them all: Casanova. The Venetian Republic, which had lasted for over a thousand years, expired in the late eighteenth century and ultimately Napoleon took our independence, our treasures, and bundled us up with the rest of Italy.

Venice's various enemies, such as the Genoese, the Turks and the French, never succeeded in violating the muddy channels of the lagoon itself. Today, however, it is the sea itself (together with the gargantuan cruise ships and tankers) that threaten us – it was our beginning and maybe it will be our end. For a thousand years, the *Magistrato alle Acque* (Magistrate for the Waters) of the Venetian Republic – in whose premises at the foot of the Rialto Bridge one can still see the coats of arms of three *Savi alle Acque* (distinguished water experts), including Girolamo da Mosto – carefully regulated the waters and activities in the lagoon. Now, in the space of just two centuries, under innumerable governments, the natural balance has been destroyed by the forces of 'advancement' and by neglect, leaving the city poised on the brink of an agonizing extinction by inundation. Venice was so beautiful and pulsed with its own life; we have failed in our love for it, abandoning it and leaving it to become little more than a showcase.

 LIVING WITH THE SEA

OPPOSITE Venice seen from the Lido with the unmistakable campaniles of San Giorgio and San Marco. Galileo demonstrated his telescopes from the top of San Marco at the end of the sixteenth century – useful also for identifying approaching boats.

The Adriatic 'system' is a term covering the network of naval communications that has brought together all the different peoples on its shores, all the way across to the Middle East; it's a lively and tumultuous set of interactions involving not only the inhabitants of several regions of Italy but also those of Central Europe. It has been operating for at least 3,000 years, supported by great fleets of ships serving commercial exchanges between the Italian Adriatic and the eastern Mediterranean, to the economic and cultural benefit of all areas. Since the days of the Phoenicians,

Sunrise over Venice.

Dawn soon comes and it's time to leave. It's still dark when I set off with Jane and the children towards the Black Swan. Everything happens too quickly: I say goodbye on the quay to the family, to Leonardo, my dear doctor friend, and to the two priests who bless the boat before its departure, then I leave them all standing in the dark blue light. Now all I can see are the hands waving. I can't make out their expressions or voices. The only sound is the wolf whistle sent out by my son Vettor; I reply in kind, as if two hands were clasped, unwilling to let go. There's a lump in my throat. Setting off in a boat is different from setting off by car or by plane, because everything happens so slowly; the goodbyes seem to go on forever, like the feelings that lie behind them.

with their superb seafaring skills, the peoples of the Mediterranean have been in constant contact with one another, spreading the gifts of civilization. The lagoon areas of the Adriatic – in Spina, then Aquileia, Venice, Caorle and Chioggia – were places where ships could shelter from the fury of the elements and from the rough seas whipped up by the fierce Bora wind. Together, they constituted a kind of interconnected protected area for navigation; at first this area was of modest proportions but subsequently it grew to connect all the Adriatic ports.

Navigation was made easier by the great number of ports along the coast, especially in Istria, Dalmatia and Albania, but also in Greece, a country that had a tradition of constant traffic between its hundreds of islands going back thousands of years. Along the Istrian coast, from Capodistria to Fiume and Lussino, there were convenient harbours every few kilometres, which provided not only mooring places for small sailing boats but also opportunities for ships to stock up on water (which would go bad on board very swiftly) and provisions such as vegetables, fruit, fish and meat of various kinds.

In the heady days of the Republic of Venice, the galleys used to go first from the Arsenale to moor in the *Bacino di San Marco* (just tens of metres from the *Black Swan*'s mooring place), where the crews would board. Amid great farewells, a mass of traffic and dense crowds, they would then be guided out of the lagoon by a pilot, who would take them out into the open sea, through the lagoon mouth of San Nicolò at the northern tip of the Lido.

After much anticipation and some trepidation the *Black Swan* is now taking me to the former colonies and along some of the Venetian trading routes. It is a journey into my city's past, as a Venetian whose ancestors used to sail this route, into my own self. Leaving the lagoon of Venice, through the same waters as my forebears, we sail past the fortress of Sant'Andrea.

If Venice were not an ex-island (now attached to the mainland by the so-called 'Ponte della Libertà' or Freedom Bridge), but something like the boat I'm sailing in, it would be freer of interference from ephemeral, unthinking governments. It would be ruled only by the necessities of its millennial coexistence with nature and with those who live here, who have always known how to master its sails.

THE FORTRESS OF SANT'ANDREA AND THE DEPTHS OF VENETIAN RESISTANCE

In the spring of 1797, the Doge declared that the fortress of Sant'Andrea's days as a defensive structure were over. However, not all its functionaries supported the decision, as is demonstrated by the chain of events immediately preceding the fateful end of the Venetian Republic.

In April 1797, Napoleon had issued orders to allow a French vessel into the port of Malamocco, but as the curiously named military ship *Liberateur d'Italie* approached San Nicolò it was attacked by two Venetian galliots. This was on the orders of the Venetian patrician Domenico Pizzamano, who was in charge of both the Lido and the Sant'Andrea fortresses, and the cogswain Bragadin (who was descended from the famous Marcantonio). Thirty-nine French sailors were taken prisoner and five were killed, including the commander. This attack, in defiance of Venice's official position, led to Pizzamano's imprisonment (at the request of Napoleon) and, together with the popular uprising provoked by the arrogant behaviour of the French army, gave the Emperor the pretext he needed to force the Venetian State to lay aside the power it had wielded for a thousand years. In one of the last sessions of the Venetian Council, in May 1797, Zan Alvise da Mosto, leader of the *Consulta*, tried again to persuade the Republic not to yield. However, events took their own course.

Almost a thousand years earlier, in the ninth century, following a bitter dispute between Charlemagne and the Byzantines, a Frankish attempt to violate the Venetian lagoon had met with less success when the Byzantines, together with the Veneti, tried to take Comacchio, south of the Venetian lagoon, together with its salt works

Charlemagne's vengeful son Pepin had set his heart on becoming master of

When completed, the architect, Sanmicheli, ordered all of the cannons ringing the fort to be fired at the same time, to test the building's robustness.

Dalmatia, in which enterprise he was encouraged by both the Patriarch and the promises of Doge Obelerio, who had meanwhile allied himself with the Franks. But when the Byzantines reoccupied Dalmatia, Obelerio capitulated to the Eastern Empire, sending the leaders of the pro-Frankish party to the Emperor as hostages, only to switch sides again and ally himself with the Franks.

As a result, Pepin asked the Venetians for naval assistance. But instead of giving it to him, Doge Obelerio and his co-regent Beato went to Charlemagne and tried to convince him that their only interest was commerce, that they loved peace and wished to be on good terms with everyone. Charlemagne greeted them with kind but vacuous words, while his son Pepin busily filled the sea with powerful naval forces. The Venetians

promptly informed the Byzantine Empire, in the hope that Nicephorus, as an ally, would come to their rescue with his fleet.

Pepin began to menace the Dalmatian ports and rivers, obstructing trade with the Venetians. The Venetians, meanwhile, set up their own defences, anchoring armed ships at the inlets to the lagoon, and smaller ships at the river mouths. They also manned the various forts erected in the lagoon. Pepin's assault proceeded swiftly, to begin with at least. Chioggia and Pellestrina were quickly overcome, sacked and burnt to the ground. The same thing happened to Eraclea and Equilio in the lagoon of Grado. At this point, Pepin paused in the southern lagoon, contemplating the difficult crossing to Malamocco, which was separated by a broad and deep channel.

The Doges voted in favour of trying to appease Pepin. However, Agnello Partecipazio, an intrepid and eloquent orator (who became the next Doge), addressed the citizens, offering first comfort to the weak and determination to the bold before thundering against the traitors in their midst, winning the hearts of the multitude in the process, who resolved to defend themselves to the last. They attacked Pepin's ships and then retreated, inviting pursuit, to the islands of Rivo Alto (Rialto) and Torcello, where the Frankish ships would find it difficult to follow them, owing to the opaque waters and tortuous inner canals. According to legend, Pepin's ships were directed towards Rivo Alto by an old lady who gave them the simple instruction '*sempre dritto*' (straight ahead) – an impossible direction in the lagoon (and indeed among the alleyways of Venice today). They were grounded on the mudflats, attacked and exterminated by the Venetians.

2

THE MARBLED COAST

Rovinj (Rovigno for the Venetians) was controlled by Venice from 1283 until 1797, when the Republic ended. Even the campanile was modelled on the one in Piazza San Marco.

 # ISTRIA

BLACK
SWAN LOG

*In the afternoon I spot land,
Istria, a thin dark line on the
horizon. For me it's like a
personal discovery but the
other members of the crew
hardly seem to notice it; maybe
they're just used to losing land
and recovering it, accustomed
as they are to living on a boat
and their everyday routines.*

WHEN I FIRST caught sight of Istria it felt like a homecomingof sorts. For it was here that, 500 years ago, my ancestors Alvise, Antonio and Benedetto da Mosto had come before me, each playing their small part in the great history of Venice's mighty Mediterranean empire. This triangular peninsula, now part of Croatia and Slovenia, remained under Venetian rule for 400 years, but its own history begins thousands of years earlier, when Venice was still an uninhabited lagoon.

Archaeological finds in southern Istria show evidence of human existence here as far back as the Paleolithic era, 800,000 years ago. But Istria derives its name from its first known settlers, the ancient Illyrian tribe of the Histri, who migrated to the area in the early Bronze Age. We know relatively little about these early inhabitants but archaeological discoveries of *situlae* – bronze vessels often decorated with scenes of day-to-day life – suggest that this was a race of skilled craftsmen with a sophisticated social structure and a keen sense of commerce. Quick to understand the strategic advantages of their location and the surrounding countryside, they created hilltop settlements surrounded by defensive walls that are still a feature of the landscape today, while also establishing far-reaching trade contacts in Greece and the Baltic region. Indeed, Istria was on one of the famous Amber Routes – an early trading network of linked roads that crossed Europe from the Baltic Sea carrying highly prized commodities such as salt and amber. The latter was not only used as jewellery and a form of currency, but was also highly prized for its legendary healing properties.

Istria's privileged location was also, perhaps, its downfall. In the second century BC the Romans, having defended the neighbouring territory of Dalmatia from marauding pirates, moved into Istria,

ABOVE Me and the main sail. OPPOSITE The Byzantine basilica of St Euphrasias in Porec (Parenzo), where Christianity was established as early as the fourth century.

31

BLACK SWAN LOG

My daughter Delia had offered me her cat, Smeraldino, for company on my voyage but Captain Giulio refused to let him come. I tried to explain that the earliest book of navigation rules, dating from the sixteenth century, said that the worst thing possible for a sailing ship was to have a 'mouse on board'.

BELOW The old street which used to lead to the Venetian *Arsenale* in Rovinj.

seeking to exploit the trading and strategic military advantages it offered. Fighting was not new to the Histri, who had already subjugated several local villages, but their warrior skills were no match for the advanced military organization of their enemy. After two bitter and bloody wars, they were defeated in 178 BC and almost sixty years later Istria was declared a colony of Rome. For the next few hundred years at least, Rome's mastery of sea and land in the area was complete.

With the collapse of the Western Roman Empire in the fifth century AD, Istria briefly came under the rule of the Eastern Roman Empire, Byzantium. But before the new administration could be fully set up, the region was thrown into turmoil by the invasion of Slavic tribes from the eastern Carpathians, who settled in the country from the seventh century onwards. The way was now paved for increasing instability and a series of changes in rulership. Over the following centuries Istria would be governed by the Franks, the Venetian Empire, the Hapsburgs, the Austrians, and, in the early twentieth century, Fascist Italy. It was later absorbed into Yugoslavia, and then, in the 1990s, divided between modern-day Slovenia and Croatia. The result of these widely varied influences is

a region in which differences in language, architecture and culture, far from being lost, have been incorporated and preserved in a spirit that is uniquely Istrian. Nowhere is this more evident than in the capital of Istria, and our first port of call, Pula.

Pula is a city and a good port and it is in a bay and there are three islands: at the tip of the bay is a church on the point and to the east is a quarry called Brancorso and it is high and rocky and wooded and the seabed offers good anchorage by the cape, sandy seabeds from 15 to 20 paces, and above the quarry at one mile towards the landfall is a tower and it is known as Orlando's tower and that is the landmark of Pula, and the tower is east of Pula.

ALVISE DA MOSTO, *PORTOLANO*, 1490

Pula (originally called Pola) sits at the southern tip of the Istrian peninsula, today part of Croatia. First settled by the Histri in the Bronze and Iron Ages, it is believed to be the oldest city in the region. There is evidence that it was known to early Greek voyagers, and it is mentioned in the ancient Greek myth of the Golden Fleece. Legend has it that when Jason, leader of the Argonauts, stole the Golden Fleece from Colchis, he escaped with his accomplice, Medea, the daughter of the king of Colchis, and took refuge from the pursuing Colchians here.

Pula, like the rest of Istria, fell under the rule of Rome, subsequently coming under a succession of different rulers. Today, more than 2,000 years later, it has a new identity as a thriving modern city with a strong industrial base and a population that is predominantly Slavic – a far cry from that small Roman port that was founded all those years ago. But to any visitor approaching Pula from the sea the initial impact it is still of the Roman legacy in the imposing form of the amphitheatre. Parallel to our boat as we sailed towards the harbour, it was an overwhelming presence, dominating the skyline. More than just a prominent landmark, however, this was, and remains, an ever-present reminder of the power and influence of the great Roman civilization.

ROMAN OCCUPATION

It is easy to see why this Adriatic town would have been so attractive to the Romans. The combination of the wide bay with its broad opening allowing easy access for ships, and the surrounding hills providing perfect shelter from the harsh Bora wind, offered excellent possibilities for trading. Today, much of the harbour is a naval base, but this was once a place where goods such as wine, oil and olives would have been loaded and transported to other Roman colonies.

The port was not the only thing that the Romans exploited. Quick to recognize the strategic advantages of the fortified hilltop settlements built by their predecessors, they did not change

BLACK SWAN LOG

In the distance I can see Pula's campanile and the great amphitheatre with its three orders of arches. Now I spot the lighthouse of Porer, which I am curious to visit, if the waves allow it, to see how people live cut off from civilization. It's a tiny isolated islet with a lighthouse in the middle, all built in Istrian stone, dazzling white in the sunlight. It stands a few miles from Pula, at the tip of the Istrian peninsula. We are approaching Pula from the south and to the north I spot the silhouette of the island of Brioni. I visited it once, a few years ago, for dinner. We were guests at an incongruously dark, wood-panelled villa, full of paintings in a gloomy but powerful Expressionist style. The villa had belolnged to Tito's finance minister, when Yugoslavia was in its heyday. We ate branzino al sale [salt-encrusted sea bass]; it was served by the minister's former manservant, prepared just the way we do it at home. The practice of cooking fish under a thick coat of salt is an ancient tradition in the Venice lagoon, where the salt pans were already functioning before the end of the Roman Empire.

BLACK SWAN LOG

Life at sea has always been a tricky business. In the days before radar and satellite navigation, thousands of man-operated lighthouses dotted the Mediterranean to help ships reach their destination safely. I jump into the dinghy with Raffaele, the captain's younger brother (whom I'll call Raffa from now on, like everyone else). We're also joined by Goga, who is technically the hostess on board, but who clearly knows as much as anyone on how to handle the sails and ropes. She speaks Croatian and can interpret for me when I meet the lighthouse keeper – a charming Bosnian man called Ivo, who has a wonderful smile. He's repairing a fishing net that stretches from the doorway of the lighthouse all the way through his apartment to the kitchen at the back. A long net to while away long hours away from his family. As we talk, he tells me about a terrible storm the lighthouse suffered in 1966 – the same storm, I realize, that struck Venice, causing the great flood that I still remember vividly, even though I was only five at the time.

them but instead adapted them to the traditional Roman grid street system. In Pula itself the castle at the top of the hill was retained as a vantage point from which to monitor and protect the bay, and the central citadel was surrounded with streets. The population expanded, trade flourished and Pula soon became an important centre on the route between Asia Minor and Aquileia, the fortified town built by the Romans in the Gulf of Trieste. So highly valued was it that between 42 and 31 BC, under the reign of the Emperor Augustus, it was elevated by the Romans to colonial status and given the title of Colonia Julia Pola Pollentia Herculanea. With that rank and title, the citizens gained certain privileges and, over the next few centuries, other symbols of status and prestige began to appear in the form of arches, a temple, an amphitheatre and theatres. All of these were made from Istrian stone, a hard-wearing local limestone that was used to create many classical antiquities and, later, Venetian houses.

Today numerous Roman relics still remain in the old town: the Hercules Gate (built in the mid-first century BC), which bears a relief carving of the mythical hero; the Arch of the Sergii (29 BC), originally a city gate commissioned by Salvia Postuma Sergia to commemorate the achievements of three members of the Sergius family at the Battle of Actium; the Temple of Augustus (2 BC–AD 14), built to celebrate the cult of the emperor and one of the finest Roman temples to have survived outside Italy; and two theatres (both first century AD). But magnificent

The gates to the Venetian fortress at Pula (Pola), built in the seventeenth century.

THE PULA AMPHITHEATRE

Pula's amphitheatre is the only remaining Roman amphitheatre to have three orders (or levels) and a complete external shell, that are intact; neither the arena of Verona nor the Colosseum in Rome has its outer perimeter anymore. It was created in the first century AD, when Pula became a regional centre of Roman rule, and was called the *Pietas Julia* (a name derived from the sand that, since antiquity, covered the inner space). For reasons of space and safety it was built outside the town walls, along the Via Flavia that went all the way to Aquileia and Rome.

The arches of the amphitheatre date from the reign of Emperor Claudius (AD 41–54); the original wooden structure had been erected around AD 7–14, during the time of Augustus, when the colony began to flourish. In AD 79 Vespasian ordered further enlargements to accommodate gladiator fights and the structure was completed three years later under Emperor Titus.

Although sometimes referred to as elliptical, the structural plan is in fact a polycentric oval; the axes measure, respectively, 132.45 and 105.10 metres while the body of the arena rises to 32.45 metres. There would have been capacity for approximately 25,000 spectators in the *cavea* (auditorium) with its 40 or so steps rising as far as the cornice between the second and third orders; beyond this were wooden steps and a loggia. The games and combat area,

The legendary Roman amphitheatre: with over 20,000 spectators and blood-curdling events, today's soccer matches are no comparison.

known as the *arena*, is still covered with sand and measures 67.95 by 41.65 metres; it is enclosed by blocks of Istrian stone.

Following Greek custom, the amphitheatre is positioned on a slope so the part facing the sea is made up of three orders and that facing the mountain has just two. The great plinths constituting the base are visible, along with two orders of arches divided by pilasters and an attic of rectangular windows. Large beams were fixed over the drainpipes to support the removable *velarii* (awnings) used to protect spectators from sun or rain. Four towers around the perimeter had cisterns containing perfumed water that could be sprinkled onto the crowd. Under the

15 entrances to the arena was a huge ditch served by elevators for beasts, people and stage sets. The Pula amphitheatre was part of the gladiator circuit, and remained in use until the fifth century, when Emperor Honorius prohibited gladiatorial combats (although it was not until 681 that combat between convicts, particularly those sentenced to death, and wild animals was also forbidden).

By this time, people had ceased to appreciate the relevance of the monument and its ironwork started to be removed for other uses, along with the bronze gateways and stone steps. At the beginning of the thirteenth century, the Patriarch of Aquileia issued severe punishments and penalties of up to 100 *bisanti d'oro* for every stone removed from the arena. Under Venetian rule, however, many of the large stones of the steps were sent to Venice to be used in the foundations of palaces. At the end of the Middle Ages the inner part of the amphitheatre was used for 'Frankish Fairs', animal grazing and horse races organized by the Knights of Malta. At the beginning of the sixteenth century, the Bolognese architect and scholar Sebastiano Serlio visited Pula and carried out measurements and drawings that were published in his treatise on architecture. In 1583 the Venetian Senator Gabriele Emo managed to suppress a proposal to deconstruct the amphitheatre piece by piece in order to rebuild it in Venice.

though each structure is in its own right, all are eclipsed by the amphitheatre, a breathtaking and extremely well preserved masterpiece built of gleaming white Istrian stone (also known as *petra d'Orsera*).

The sixth largest amphitheatre in the world, and believed to be even older than the Colosseum in Rome, the Pula arena was built under the reign of the Emperor Vespasian with a very special kind of mass entertainment in mind. Of all the forms of institutionalized cruelty throughout human history, the Roman Games are the most notorious. Although ostensibly a way of hardening Roman citizens to help them to endure wars better, this was murder on a vast scale for pure pleasure. Typically, the games would begin with the slaughter of hundreds of wild, often rare animals. These were brought from increasingly far-flung places to satisfy an ever-demanding crowd, and were often pitted against criminals or Christians for the public's entertainment. As each batch of men and animals was led out into the amphitheatre, others waited in the underground corridors to meet their fate in the arena of death above. The stench – of animal dung, dried blood and fear – must have been terrible. Yet all this was just a preamble to the main act: the gladiators, professional fighters specially trained to perform in the arena, either in single combat or in teams.

Although the name 'gladiator' comes from the Latin word *gladius*, meaning sword; in reality gladiators fought with a variety of weapons, and were broadly classified into four main types: the *murmillo*, who fought with a helmet, oblong shield and sword, and had the crest of a fish on his helmet; the *retarius*, armed with a net and trident; the *Samnite*, with an oblong shield, visored helmet and sword, and the *Thracian*, who had a round shield and curved scimitar.

Most gladiators were condemned prisoners, criminals or slaves and the fight was often to the death. For those who were successful, however, there was the potential to obtain fame, fortune and even the adoration of women (although, contrary to popular opinion, gladiators were not only men – the poet Publius Statius, writing in the first century, also mentions women). The temptation of adulation was so great that many freemen volunteered to fight in the arena. Repeatedly successful gladiators were sometimes able to gain their freedom, but ultimately the fate of all such fighters rested on the will of the Emperor and the people. When a gladiator was defeated, thumbs up from the crowd indicated a recommendation for life; thumbs down was the signal for death. This made ordinary people equal with the Emperor, by putting the power of life and death into their hands – literally.

The custom of gladiatorial combat seems to have originated with the Etruscans, and was introduced by the Romans in 264 BC, initially solely for public funerals. But the craze soon caught on, reaching its peak at the height of the Empire, and eventually degenerating into wholesale butchery. The games were finally banned in AD 325 by the Emperor Constantine,

ISTRIAN STONE

Istrian stone is a type of limestone formed during the Cretaceous period and has been highly valued since ancient times. Its marble-like appearance has made it highly desirable for the creation of magnificent structures, not least the amphitheatre in Pula.

The stone was well known in the Roman age, when ships were already plying regularly between the Adriatic ports and the Middle East. This traffic had existed since the fourth century with the early Veneti and the civilization of Spina, an ancient city (originally Etruscan, then Greek and subsequently Gallic) at the mouth of the Po, north-west of today's Comacchio. Transportation from the Istrian shore was complicated as although the weight of the stones stabilized the ships, open-sea voyages were considered riskier and more demanding than coasting, which remained the usual practice until the middle of the nineteenth century. Particularly heavy blocks of stone – such as the massive one that covers the mausoleum of Theodoric in Ravenna – had to be moved on huge rafts, which were tied to ships.

Venice used Istrian stone from the second half of the thirteenth century, as we can see from the bases of the columns of St Mark and St Theodore in St Mark's Square. Its use in construction and decoration increased following the Venetian conquest of the ports of Parenzo and Capodistria. Throughout the fourteenth and fifteenth centuries it was used mainly to create statues, decorative features, cornices, doorposts, frames and gutters, but in later years, as the quarries were enlarged to meet rising Venetian demands, it came to be used for columns, pillars, entire façades and architraves.

Work in the quarries was very rewarding, if extremely tiring; for many centuries it was also the main local source of income for hundreds of workers. The Venetians paid their quarrymen and masons handsomely for their work so while it is true that Venice owes a great deal to Istria for its contribution to her palaces, it could also be said that the

---

The Arch of Balbi, Rovinj, with its gregarious fifteenth-century lion in an ornamental structure from 1680.

economy of the area around Rovinj (Rovigno), where the stone of Orsera came from, flourished in large part thanks to the continued demand from Venice.

The Venetian Republic, usually via the Council of Ten, regulated the profits from the quarries and mines in its territories, but as early as 1307 Venice had a body of laws governing the art of the stone-cutters, and from 1440 onwards the *Provveditori al Sal* (government superintendents) oversaw the importation of Istrian stone from Rovinj. According to statistics from the end of the seventeenth century there were 4,000 quarries in the area around Rovinj, Albona and Fialona. These, for the most part, extracted stone for cutting and carving; smaller pieces became lime and gravel for various uses, including roadbeds in the vicinity.

The largest and finest quarries were in Orsera and Rovinj, but records also mention Gradina, Signori, Mondelao and Salina. The quarry of Orsera, in particular, was very well situated in the hills sloping down to the sea – this made it easier to transport the stone to the ports. The quarry is a remarkable sight, especially with the white cathedral bell tower in the background. The stone here is of very high quality, compact and ivory white in colour. The strata are exceptionally thick – the ideal prerequisite for creating monumental columns and pillars. The system of quarries south of the small town of Rovinj was larger than in Orsera and provided over half a million cubic metres of stone over 300 years.

Lovely examples of the Venetian Gothic style linger throughout Istria; together with the geraniums, it feels like home.

 BLACK SWAN LOG

Day two on the Black Swan and I get up early to help Massimo do the shopping. Wandering the streets, he is lost in thought about what to cook, while I am reminded of our long historical links with this place: there are still coats of arms of Venetian families on the buildings and doorways. My mind wonders back to something my grandfather Andrea said half-ironically – that 'nothing would be easier' with the documents of the Archive of the Frari, where the archives of the Serenissima are preserved, than to re-establish, today, the government of the extinct Republic of St Mark, with its Doge, its Senate, even its Council of Ten (and I think there would be a need for it again), and its complicated administrative machinery, its prerogatives, its laws, its bonds, its laxities, and, why not, just to complete the illusion, even its wigs and the black clothes of its patriciate'.

but did not finish until the reign of Honorius more than 60 years later. I cannot even imagine how many thousands – tens of thousands – of people died in the arena at Pula in its 400 years of activity. Today it is used for much gentler forms of mass entertainment such as operas and concerts, where the audience has the rare pleasure of glimpsing snatches of deep blue sea through magisterial Roman arches while listening to the music.

THE SPIRIT OF VENICE

In addition to mirroring the history of Rome, there is another story of Pula to be told, that of a city soaked in the spirit of Venice. In the thirteenth century, Istria, and Pula with it, fell to the Venetian empire, and over the 500 years that followed, Venice left its inimitable mark on the city. This was a time of renewal and revival, when Romanesque campaniles were recreated in Gothic style and loggias (still used as covered markets here) appeared everywhere. As trade flourished, the wealth of local merchants increased, and Venetian Gothic palazzi were built.

ABOVE AND OPPOSITE
In Motovun, the many lion
symbols of the Venetian
colonizers take various
forms: *in moleca* (above, left
and right) is when the lion's
head is surrounded by wings
and looks like the Venetian
crab (*moleca*); *andante* (above,
centre) is when he advances
intrepidly; and when he has
the book closed (above,
centre and right) it means he
is ready to fight. Another lion
can be found on the gateway
to the castle (opposite).

OVERLEAF Main portal of
Motovun, built by the
Venetians.

Over the years, temples became churches, forums became squares or *campi*, and grandeur began to be replaced by the small-scale intimacy that is so distinctively Venetian.

Walking through the narrow medieval streets, I spotted a da Mosto emblem and was reminded of my rascally ancestor Antonio, who was tried in 1661 for his irregular administration of this city. The *fondaco* (market) was mismanaged, orders from the Most Excellent magistrates of the Dalmatian coast were often ignored, and he cultivated strange acquaintances. He was on good terms with notorious criminals who had been banished for smuggling, and in a number of cases he was even, disgracefully, persuaded by money or gifts to turn a blind eye to minor crimes.

It is shameful that he didn't show more respect for his forebear Benedetto da Mosto, who had been *podesta* of Portole, a town in the centre of the Istrian peninsula, a century earlier. Benedetto commemorated his family and celebrated the justice and impartiality of his mandate by erecting a massive symbol of Venetian power in the town: a winged lion complete with the da Mosto coat of arms, quartered in gold and silver, and the inscription BENEDICTUS DE MUSTO PRAETOR POSUIT MDXXVIII. This monumental sculpture, which weighed one-and-a-half tons, didn't seem to have made much of an impression on his successors!

Far be it from me to excuse the behaviour of my relatives, but the sad truth is that Antonio was simply a product of his times. From the fourteenth century onwards, Venice became too weakened by its struggle against the neighbouring state of Genoa to maintain control of Pula and by the sixteenth century the city was already in decline. By the mid-seventeenth century, political difficulties and a series of plagues had left Pula a ghost town, with a population of only 300, compared to its peak of 30,000 under Roman rule. In 1866 it was taken over by the Austrian empire, and then in 1918 by the Italian Fascists, before finally becoming part of modern-day Croatia. In 1904, Irish writer James Joyce lived in Pula for a short period, working as a teacher. The charms of the town were lost on him, and in his letters home he referred to it as a 'naval Siberia'.

ISTRIA & MY RELATIVES

My family has had a connection with Istria since the 1600s. Giacomo was praetor in Rovigno (Rovinj), a safe port and important stopover for Venetian ships hugging the Istrian coast on their way to the Orient. This ancestor still gazes down at us from a portrait, wearing a white wig and a red cloak, as was the custom for Venetian noblemen at the beginning of the eighteenth century.

My great-great-grandfather Andrea also spent time in Istria, first in the customs house and then working in the timber trade. The region was even more important for my great-grandfather Antonio who, after a long career in the Austrian administration, was appointed District Captain in Parenzo in 1866, where his son Andrea spent his childhood.

I never met my grandfather, who died at the age of 92 the year before I was born, but my father told me he had felt great nostalgia for those Istrian years and his Hungarian great-grandmother, Sarolta Gezy. He fondly recalled her tenderness, despite a life marked by drama worthy of a nineteenth-century novel. Talking through her tears, in French, one day she told Andrea about the tragic heartbreak she had suffered as a girl. When she came out into society as a young Hungarian in Vienna, attending the balls at the Imperial court of Franz Josef, she had fallen head over heels in love with a minor officer of the Hussars who was a divine dancer of waltzes.

The family soon got to hear of the romance, but the rules governing the behaviour of Hungarian noble families were very strict: the officer, an attractive young man full of hopes for the future, was not from a noble family, so Sarolta's parents forbade the two lovers to continue the relationship. The officer was crushed and in a moment of deep despondency killed himself with a bullet to the chest. Sarolta, overwhelmed by grief, managed to persuade her lover's family to give her the Hussar's jacket with

Giacomo da Mosto as I've always known him, a portrait hanging in the *salotto rosso*.

the bullet-hole, which she always kept in a small wooden chest. My grandfather was given the chest in memory of his beloved great-grandmother; and when my father, out of curiosity, asked about the hole in the jacket, he heard the story that had tormented his great-great-grandmother. (For the record, she later married a noble Hungarian, Augusto Palasky, since life had to go on.)

My grandfather's family had a peaceful time in Istria. He often travelled to Vienna to talk to functionaries of the Empire. He was also Chamberlain to the Court, and would be received promptly and warmly by the Emperor in person, as the 'Austrian Empire's Venetian'. He was considered one of the most handsome men in Vienna and his perfect German, spoken with a blend of the soft Viennese accent and Venetian cadences, helped to open doors. Very tall, he had a certain lordly elegance so that he was able to look

benignly down on his interlocutors among the highest ranks of Viennese society; a number of aristocratic ladies flirted openly with him, although he responded with nothing more than broad smiles, remaining firmly faithful to his wife Carlotta. (I must confess to having worn his uniform to a fancy dress party, hoping to attain the same degree of attention, but instead I had to creep away soon after dancing began as all the ancient stitching began to disintegrate!)

Antonio's career had begun soon after he graduated in Law at Padua, shortly after the Venetian uprising of 1848–9. As a patriot he had served in the civic guard during the Republic of Manin at the age of 18, and had donated all the family silver to the Republic to help the city resist against Austria, even though his father had many friends among the Austrians.

Yet when the Austrians returned, thanks to his good relations with the Court, Andrea managed to get his son into the administrative service. When the third War of Independence broke out in 1866 he was running the Austrian administration of Verona; it was then that Venice and the Veneto were finally ceded, in accordance with agreements between France and the Austrian Empire. Italy had lost two major battles: in the land battle, at Custoza, a division of Hungarian Hussars, commanded by one of his future Hungarian relatives, Augusto Bartakovich of Kis Appon, had swept down on horseback from one of the hills onto the Italian fusiliers. In the sea battle, at Lissa, as someone put it, 'the iron heads with wooden ships had beaten the iron ships with wooden heads'. During the negotiations between the Italian government and the Austrian Empire my great-grandfather opted for continuing his service to the Austrian Empire, to the great sorrow of his father Andrea, who was very fond of his son who would now live far away.

The fortified fourteenth-
century hill town of
Motovun in northern Istria,
surrounded by vineyards
and a fertile valley.

THE FERTILE HINTERLAND

Just north of Pula, in a small town called Vodjnan, the church of St Blaise has a strange
connection with Venice. It has become home to the mummified bodies of saints that were
brought here from the church of San Lorenzo in the Castello district of Venice for safe keeping,
due to imminent war, in 1818.

The curate led me behind a red curtain at the back of the altar to inspect a row of glass cases
containing many dried-up bodies, some still dressed in faded finery. These were people who had
once breathed, laughed and cried, I thought, as the priest formally introduced them to me, like
the host of a cocktail party: Leon Bembo the Blessed, a twelfth-century Venetian ambassador to
Syria, who gave up worldly pleasures to become a faith healer; St Ivan Olini, a priest who had
fearlessly exposed himself to infection when treating victims of the plague in Venice; and fellow
nun St Nikolaza de Koper (still wearing a garland of flowers around her head). She performed
many miracles including her own everlasting preservation – although she had never been
embalmed, 500 years later, her skin is still flexible (so the priest said)!

Not all of the saints were fortunate enough to have been preserved whole, however. Here, too, in small glass cabinets, were the leg of St Barbara, and the torso and arm of St Sebastian (the one who the Romans shot full of arrows). I asked if there was anything of Judas Iscariot, as he has always fascinated me. The answer was no. Judas, the priest pointed out gently but firmly, was not regarded as one of the apostles. It was a disappointing answer. I have always been interested in Judas and when I think about it, I feel a little sorry for him – after all, someone had to betray Jesus. Has anyone ever thought that, if Christ had not been betrayed, and subsequently crucified, Christianity as we know it might not exist today?

All the way back, I kept thinking about one particular relic I had seen, which had not seemed particularly significant at the time. It was a small sheet that had apparently been used to wrap Jesus when he was just a month old. When I first saw it, it had reminded me of something, but I couldn't remember what. Now, on the road back, I realized what it was. The small geometric pattern of red and white squares on the sheet was exactly the same as that on the Croatian flag. Could this symbol of national independence really have been inspired by that small piece of cloth?

Given the fact that they were brought here for safe keeping and Venice is a pretty secure city now, I wonder if they will ever be returned. The priest replies that no one has ever asked for them, and besides, they've been here for nearly 200 years so it would be a shame to disturb them again.

I came across death – and Venice – again in the chapel of Our Lady on the Rock, a small Gothic church at the top of a hill just outside the village of Beram. Guarded by a solitary cypress tree at its entrance, this seemingly humble place of worship has a coffered ceiling and contains some of the most beautiful sacred art in the region – a series of stunning fifteenth-century frescos that line its walls in shades of faded rose, green and gold. There are more than 40 scenes here, depicting episodes in the life of the Virgin Mary and Christ. This, the key-holder to the chapel explained, was the 'Bible of the Poor'. Here, in this tiny room, people who could not read or write would marvel as they learned about the lives of the saints and the stories of the New Testament.

Reminders of the bigger issues of life and death are portrayed over the entrance of the

A fresco in the chapel, showing Jesus entering Jerusalem. The cloaks of his followers line the way.

THE DANCE OF DEATH

The painting of the Dance of Death in Beram is one of many representations of the concept of the universality of death that was prevalent in medieval times. Expressed in all art forms including drama, music and poetry, the allegory typically showed Death personified in some form, leading a procession of figures from all walks of life to their graves in a macabre dance. The explicit message – death comes to us all – was a warning against vanity. As such, it underlined the ultimate irrelevance of earthly goods, and was meant to serve as a reminder of the need to prepare oneself spiritually for the inevitable.

Although the concept originated long before, it really took hold in the late Middle Ages, when it captured the mood of the times. This was a dark period in history: life was short, even at the best of times, and the devastation of the Black

Death in the mid-fourteenth century, combined with the Hundred Years' War between France and England, led to an increasing obsession with mortality. The ever-present possibility of death evoked a two-fold response: on one hand, the religious desire for penitence, and on the other a frenzied desire for last-minute enjoyment and pleasure – in short, a last dance. The Dance of Death (*danse macabre* in French or *danza de la muerte* in Spanish) seemed to satisfy both needs.

In this scene (set appropriately against a gruesome blood-red background) there are ten 'dancers', including a pope, a cardinal, a bishop,

a king (bearing a sceptre with lilies), a queen, an innkeeper, a child, a maimed man, a knight and finally – standing by a table covered with riches – a merchant. Recognized as a masterpiece of Gothic art, the artist broke many of the conventional rules of the genre. The skeletons seem to be walking rather than dancing; they are not wearing the usual shrouds, but are naked, and some of them are playing music. And although the characters come from all walks of life, they are not shown in descending order of rank or social hierarchy: the laymen are separated from the clerics, and the innkeeper, child and maimed man come immediately after the king and queen, and before the knight. In a final, chilling touch, the greedy merchant seems to be reluctant to relinquish his material wealth, in the hope, perhaps, of buying an escape from death.

chapel: for example, the Wheel of Fortune and the greatest masterpiece of all, the Dance of Death. This latter scene depicts grinning skeletons leading a procession of people to their death: people from different professions, old and young, rich and poor are all being carried away. Death is the great leveller!

These frescos, painted in 1454, are the work of brothers Vincent and Ivan of Kastav, citizens of the Venetian Republic who settled in the region. The influence of the nascent Italian Renaissance can be seen in the emotions of the some of the faces, but the naïve Slavic folk style dominates. The blending seen in these frescos forms part of an Istrian tradition of painting in which a variety of foreign influences were merged into an often rustic, but totally individual, style. And it seems to me that it is this wonderful amalgamation of cultures that both sums up the history and captures the essence of Istria. Pondering this question on the way back to the *Black Swan*, I asked my driver whether he felt Croat or Slav. It took him just one second to answer, with an unmistakable note of pride, 'Istrian. This part of Croatia, Istria, has a strong sense of identity; everyone's ruled us, and when the boss is always changing, you just have to get on with things.'

In the meantime I receive a text message from Jane on my mobile phone, giving me news of the last people I saw as we sailed away from Venice: 'When you disappeared behind Sant'Elena, the children went to the beach, Leonardo went to work at the hospital, the priests are still praying and I'm distracting myself as best I can…I'll miss you enormously but I'll cope, and meanwhile you enjoy yourself as much as possible. xxx J.' But immediately the shipping news brings me back to reality: 'Adriatic: tomorrow the weather will be mainly very hot and sunny. Winds mainly north and north-east, from moderate to strong.'

All the frescos in the tiny chapel had been painted over and were only rediscovered in 1913.

3
A CLASH ∞ OF CULTURES

View of the mountainous
Dalmatian coast from Jelsa,
on the island of Hvar.

BLACK SWAN LOG

After only a few days at sea, I am already overcome by reminders of our mortality - human relics, arenas of death, crumbling palaces and other memento mori. We're all locked into the cycle of life! It's sobering, so I am pleased to have a little fun. Like Diocletian's Palace at its heart, Split is not only a museum, but a living city where the people have their own way of doing things. A sandy beach in the heart of the city, Bacvice, is the Spalatines' favourite place. Its shallow water is perfect for playing the famous game picigin, using a small ball and the palm of the hand as a racquet. The crew of the Black Swan and I join a local enthusiast, Ante: 'No teams and no points, we're not interested in winners or losers, he explains, 'The idea is just to keep the ball up in the air.' But then he qualifies himself by saying his team are the world champions! Antisa, a friend of Ante's with a big moustache, slaps his stomach proudly and adds: 'If you don't want to get hurt when you jump for the ball it's best to have a good belly, for padding.'

A street in Split that clearly recalls the days of Venetian dominion.

under Turkish rule and the whole of the Aegean Sea was swarming with belligerent fleets. Giovanni da Mosto was *castellano* (chatelain) in Split in 1461 when the Venetian army attacked the Turks in Rhodes. The same army was later defeated at Patras by the Turks, who then pushed their way into the Adriatic. Giovanni returned to Venice to advise the city of the land movements of the approaching Ottomans, who, ten years later, had advanced to within a hundred kilometres of Venice.

Other ancestors did not fare as well. Andrea, *castellano* on the nearby island of Traù (Trogir), died there in 1558, a long way from his city, his family and beloved wife, who at least was supported by the State: she received 266 ducats, 14 *denari* and 12 *piccoli* from the salary owing to him. His great-grandson Lorenzo, captain in Zara (Zadar) for about three years until 1762, also lost his life in service and his children were also granted a pension by the Republic.

These stories are tiny events when set against the ancient history of Split. Sailing into the harbour on that beautiful summer's morning, there was no mistaking the still powerful presence of Rome. The campanile I had seen was that of St Domius Cathedral, formerly Diocletian's mausoleum, just a tiny part of the vast remains of the Emperor Diocletian's palace.

ABOVE, LEFT A Corinthian capital from Jupiter's Temple: more Roman remains at the heart of modern Split.
ABOVE, RIGHT Turks in a humbling sculptural representation in Trogir Cathedral. (Another column has some Jews in the same predicament).
OPPOSITE The Romanesque campanile of Split Cathedral, seen through the columns of the Roman peristyle of Diocletian's Palace.

THE *GONFALONE* OF ST MARK

The earliest *gonfalone* or banner of the Republic of Venice probably consisted of a golden cross on a sky-blue field, the colours of the Byzantine Empire to which the city formally belonged. Evidence for this can be found in a panel of the exceptionally rich altar screen in St Mark's Basilica, known as the 'Pala d'Oro', which was assembled by Venetian goldsmiths in the fourteenth century. It is made up of jewel-encrusted enamel panels, one of which depicts the relics of St Mark being received into the basilica, where a soldier holds a standard with the same symbol of a golden cross.

Earlier, conflicting, evidence of a Venetian standard was provided in 998 by the historian Giovanni Diacono who stated that, setting off on a naval expedition against the Narentines, the Bishop of Olivolo consigned to Doge Pietro Orseolo II a triumphal standard featuring the lion of St Mark.

Without a doubt, once the body of St Mark the Evangelist had been brought to the city and adopted as Venice's patron saint, it became the custom to show banners emblazoned with the lion of St Mark on a blue field rimmed with crosses and gold decorations on a red band. Thus the lion began its life as a political emblem on the flags and standards of the Republic during the first half of the thirteenth century.

In the mosaics of the chapel of St Isidore, also in the basilica, which date from 1355 and show the transportation in 1125 of the body of St Isidore from the island of Chios by Doge Domenico Michiel, the island's fortress is depicted, together with a quayside and some galleys. Various flags are shown flying on the towers of the fortress, on the poles holding the lamps along the quayside and on the stern of the ship. On each flag is a lion *in moleca* (in the form of a 'crab' – that is, the lion's head with wings on either side).

In official ceremonies and processions involving the Doge, the standard itself was preceded by eight *comandatori* (representatives of the law), who all held white, red, blue and violet standards of St Mark. Only the navy's flags were red, as were their uniforms. This is why the standards raised on the poles in Piazza San Marco have always been red, because the poles represented – and originally were – ships' masts.

Here the *gonfalone* shows the winged lion ready for battle with one paw on the closed book and the other brandishing a sword

In times of peace, the lion was shown with his right front paw resting on an open copy of the Gospel bearing the words PAX TIBI MARCE EVANGELISTA MEUS (Peace to you, Mark, my Evangelist). This was the phrase spoken by an angel to the Bishop of Alexandria (Egypt) when he came to the lagoon after a shipwreck, heralding the fact that his mortal remains would come to rest in that part of the world, where a great city would rise. But when the city was at war, the lion was shown with his paw resting on a closed book, or on an open book without words, and clutching a sword. The lion with the open book was intended to show the world that the Republic's actions were governed by culture and knowledge. The closed book and sword made it clear that when the city was at war other considerations took precedence.

Recently, the cultural association European Identity organized a re-enactment of the Venetians' famous victory under the command of Sebastiano Venier at the Battle of Lepanto in 1571. It was a modest event prepared by young people who are passionate about their history and cultural heritage, and who devote their free time to the rediscovery of traditional cultural values that would otherwise be lost. However, as they were about to raise the *gonfalone* of St Mark, which is also the banner of the Veneto Region, a zealous official from the town council blocked the ceremony, due to a regulation that prohibits the *gonfalone* from being raised unless it is together with the European and Italian flags!

Hvar Cathedral reflects the architectural principles governing the design of San Michele and San Zaccaria in Venice, where the line across the upper curves of the façade represents the ideal horizon.

 BLACK SWAN LOG

From Split, we sail towards the cluster of beautiful islands off the coast of Croatia – the 'Caribbean' of the Adriatic, judging by the number of people, especially Italians, who sail here every summer. It's night-time and Giulio is at the helm, keeping watch. The stars are shining brightly so to make conversation, I tell Giulio about my ancestor Alvise, the first Westerner to describe the Southern Cross, when he was navigating the southern waters of Senegal near the River Gambia in the mid-fifteenth century.

CONFLICT AND RESOLUTION

One of a cluster of beautiful islands off the coast of Dalmatia, Hvar was originally settled by the Greeks before falling under Roman, then Byzantine, control. For centuries Hvar town was overrun with pirates until the Venetians drove them out in the thirteenth century and encouraged inhabitants of other parts of the island to resettle here. In 1420, when Dalmatia was ceded to *La Serenissima*, the Venetians returned and stayed, eager to take hold of this strategic location on the trade route between Venice and the East.

BLACK SWAN LOG

Hvar island is Croatia's party capital; sitting at a bar with some of the crew and a bottle of wine we start by surveying what the evening might have in store. But before making elaborate plans, we remind ourselves that life on the Black Swan starts early, no matter what happened the night before, so we end up playing an old game that I learned at sea: 'the quarter-dollar'. You place a glass in the middle of a sturdy wood table, then you flip a quarter, or any other single-alloy coin that bounces well, trying to get it into the glass. When it goes in, you choose someone to make drink a glass of wine in a single swig. Then you do the 'drop test' on the glass: turning it upside-down, if a single drop comes out the victim has to drink another full glass!

ABOVE Weather-beaten fifteenth century lions linger in Hvar .

OPPOSITE Layers of architecture like stage sets reflect the levels of Venetian influence in this region, from simple domestic architecture to the Gothic and military styles on Hvar.

In the years that followed the island experienced a financial, cultural and architectural boom. The fifteenth-century Venetian citadel, with its sturdy towers and lion of St Mark, is still here, but the gift of our architecture cannot, sadly, be considered compensation for the oppression suffered under the Venetians – a disgraceful episode in our history.

During this period of Venetian rule, the nobility had ultimate sovereignty and by the fifteenth century the locals had been completely excluded from government and deprived of any form of power. So in 1510, Matija Ivanić led a revolt, sacking the houses of the nobles and killing their inhabitants. After weeks of chaos the Venetian navy arrived, and a shameful massacre took place; the surviving rebels were hanged from the masts of the Venetian ships, for all to see. Tensions simmered long after. Resolution eventually came from the most unexpected quarter – the backbone of the island's oppression, the Arsenale, where Venetian weapons and warships were kept. It was here, in 1612, that the Venetian governor of the time, Pietro Semitecolo, had an unusual idea of how to improve relations between the nobility and commoners. By adapting the upper storey to house a theatre, he believed that people could get to know each other better in the pursuit of a common interest, and thus end the fighting. The oldest indoor theatre in Croatia and one of the oldest in Europe, it is still in use today.

A Franciscan monastery on the outskirts of Hvar town tells another story of enlightened Venetian thinking. In 1461 a Venetian sea captain, making a journey along a similar route to mine, was saved from a shipwreck and, in thanks to God, he used his wealth to found a monastery to take care of the sick, especially shipwreck survivors. It was also a quarantine station for sailors returning from the further territories of the Venetian Empire.

 THE MOSTAR BRIDGE

It's just a day's drive inland from Split, yet many people don't think of Bosnia and Herzegovina as a Mediterranean country. Its coastline is just a few kilometres long but it has played a

The recently restored Mostar bridge, made exactly as it was before and using many of the old stones salvaged from the river.

significant role in the history of this region. I decided to visit the town of Mostar not only because of the famous bridge that became a symbol of struggle and survival during the horrors of the Balkans conflicts but also on a quest for the possible origin of my name. *Mustes* referred to the ancient priests who were initiated in the Mysteries, and was an eponym for Bacchus or Dionysius, the god of wine, which also comes from *mosto* – must. And in Slavonic languages, from the Balkans to Poland, ancient Thrace to Dacia on the Caspian Sea, *most* means bridge.

Five hundred years ago, the Dinaric Alps mountain range running parallel to the Adriatic coast was the frontline of the Turkish Ottoman advance as they approached from Istanbul intent on conquering Western Europe. But these mountains were as far as they got, and ever since then the mountains have represented a division that runs through this region: people inland have tended to be Muslims, while those on the coastal side have remained Christian. The two groups have mostly lived together peacefully, but in times of trouble the cultural fault line is quick to appear – something it didn't take long for me to be reminded of. After travelling a few kilometres inland, I stopped at a bridge to admire the landscape and there, at the side of the

road, next to a river, was a marble tombstone. Decorated with red and white plastic flowers and a photograph of a boy in uniform, it bore the simple inscription: 'Željko Kukrika 1971–1992' – a poignant reminder of the suffering this area has seen.

Today the town is still divided in two, reflecting the historic dualism of the region. East of the Neretva river that flows through the town there are mosques and hammams, while on the western side there are churches. It looked peaceful enough on the day I was there, but in 1993, during the Bosnian civil war, the old divisions erupted, and the main boulevard, now lined with bombed-out buildings, became the battle frontline: Muslims on one side, Christians on the other.

The greatest symbol of the Balkans conflict was the destruction of the bridge, built in 1566 by order of the Sultan Suleiman the Magnificent soon after the Ottomans captured the area. Replacing a rickety wooden suspension bridge, the stone bridge was meant to symbolize a new unity between East and West. The single arch spanning 27 metres is an engineering masterpiece and since it was built it has been customary for young men of all creeds to leap from the bridge to prove their manhood. Destroyed during the 1993 civil war, this symbol of harmony and national identity was one of the rebuilding priorities and since 2004 young Christians and Muslims have been able to gather here again, to put history behind them and leap into a hopeful future.

Despite the recent influx of tourism, traces of suffering and sadness still linger here. Many buildings outside the tourist area remain half-destroyed and half-inhabited, their walls pockmarked with bullet holes. Seeing these scars on interior walls reminds me that fighting

ABOVE, LEFT Many shelled buildings linger beyond the tourist circuit in Mostar.
ABOVE, TOP RIGHT In Bosnia, a memorial to a young soldier rests as a reminder of our fragility amid a verdant landscape.
ABOVE, BELOW RIGHT Now, as they have done for centuries, the young men of Mostar jump from the bridge to prove their manhood.

NICOLÒ, MATTEO AND MARCO POLO AT THE COURT OF KUBLA KHAN

Around 1262, when Nicolò and Matteo Polo returned to the court of Kubla, Great Khan of the Western Tartars, they took Nicolò's son Marco with them. He was welcomed into the ruler's family and proved so eager to learn the customs and languages of the Tartars that Kubla entrusted him with important tasks. During the next seventeen years, Marco was sent on several missions, visiting most of Asia and places that no European had ever been. When he returned, he gave detailed reports to the ruler of what he had seen of the customs and other activities. Kubla greatly appreciated all this and came to esteem the Polos highly.

However, after all this time away from home the three Venetians had become nostalgic. They asked Kubla for his permission to return to Venice, but he bore such love towards them that he could never bring himself to grant it. In the meantime, the Bulgarian queen, wife of Argon, Lord of the Levant (Persia) died. Since only women of the same lineage could sit on the throne, Argon sent three of his barons to Kubla, to request another bride of the same lineage as the dead queen. The Great Khan accordingly nominated a seventeen-year-old girl named Cocacin. The envoys accepted Kulba's choice and prepared to set out with her.

Nervous about undertaking the long journey overland, they had been thinking about taking her home by sea. At that moment, Marco Polo arrived back from a long sea voyage to the Indies, so Argon's barons asked Kubla another favour – the Polos' enjoyable company and knowledge of the coasts and seas, to escort them home. Their wish was granted, on condition the Polos promised to come back to Kubla's court.

Before leaving, the Great Khan summoned all three Polos and gave them two golden tablets, which would allow them to travel freely throughout his kingdom. He also charged them to take

Part of Marco Polo's house in Korcula, if it's true that he or his family ever lived here.

embassies to the Pope, to the kings of France, England and Spain, as well as to other Christian kings along the way. He also gave them fourteen ships, fully supplied and provisioned for two years.

The Polos set off together with Argon's envoys and the young Cocacin, as well as the daughter of the King of the Mangi, whom Kubla had asked the Polos to escort to Tabris. After many months they reached the court of Argon, but the king had meanwhile passed away, so the beautiful young Cocacin married his son, Cazan, instead. The queen was sad to have to bid farewell to the Polos; she saw them almost as fathers and wept when they departed on horseback.

From Tabris they travelled to Trebizond and then to Constantinople, and from there sailed to Negropont in Greece and finally arrived in Venice in 1295, more than three-and-a-half years after leaving the court of Kubla. Eager to recount their

adventures, the Polos were not welcomed at first; their relatives and fellow citizens could barely recognize them after so long away and they looked so different, both in their features and their clothes; even their language had changed, after talking so long to the Tartars.

Marco had little time to relax as another war was breaking out between the Venetians and the Genoese for dominion over the seas. A fleet of 60 Venetian galleys was roving the Mediterranean, seeking to intimidate her enemies. So Genoa equipped an even larger and stronger fleet, composed of 85 galleys, and sent it to the Adriatic. On hearing this news, Venice assembled 95 ships, manned by its most valiant citizens, and entrusted the supreme command to Andrea Dandolo. Marco Polo enrolled, eager to defend his homeland. On 8 September 1298, the two fleets met in the waters of Korcula; and this time Genoa won. Only 16 Venetian galleys were saved. Dandolo, badly wounded, was chained to the mainmast of his own ship, and Marco Polo, also wounded, was captured.

As the victorious fleet approached Genoa, the tumultuous cheering of the crowds on the quays together with war trumpets and bell-ringing made such a din that the wretched Dandolo could not bear the humiliation. In despair, he moved as far as his chains would allow him and dashed his brains out against the mast.

The prisons of Genoa were opened to receive the Venetian prisoners. Marco Polo found himself in a cell with a Pisan prisoner named Rusticiano (captured 14 years earlier in the battle of Meloria) and they became great friends. Polo recounted his adventures to Rusticiano, who wrote them up in the famous account of his travels. When peace was made between Venice and Genoa in 1299, Marco returned home where he finally lived a life of leisure until his death in 1323.

wasn't by way of cold, impersonal bombs; rather each hole was created by someone deliberately shooting to kill another person in that place. Not even the balcony of my hotel room was intact: the white-tiled floor and the metal base of the window frame had numerous marks made by single bullets, fired from a rifle or a small-calibre machine-gun. The balcony of the next room was pristine so I presume my room held a sniper who had to be eliminated.

STORYTELLING

This green, pine-covered island was first settled by the Greeks, who called it Corcyra Melaina ('Black Corfu') because of its dark mass of woodland. As we approached, however, it was the rocks and walls of Korcula (Curzola in Venetian times) that were the most prominent, descending almost to the water's edge, with the mountains in the distance. My ancestor Zan Alvise was made *Conte di Curzola* in the mid-sixteenth century. His posting lasted seven months and seventeen days and during his rule municipal wells were dug for the inhabitants. Before coming here, however, I'd never heard the story that Marco Polo was born in Korcula town.

It's now early morning: I painfully remember last night as I hear my name being shouted. There's only one thing worse than a hangover – and that's a hangover at sea! A sailing boat nearby is putting out and we watch them as they pull up the anchor; today Agostino, the mechanic, has been working on the engines of the anchors all morning. Lorenzo, after half a day off, is in the shade smoothing down the deck, while, Beppe, tireless as ever, is on the alert.

Korcula town on the island of the same name, about halfway between Split and Dubrovnik.

ABOVE LEFT Sculpture by a
local artist representing the
Korculan struggle against
the Venetians.
ABOVE RIGHT A detail from
Korcula Cathedral.
OPPOSITE The courtyard of a
Venetian house in Korcula
town.

Like most other Venetians, I had always believed he was born in Venice. Yet papers from the local archives seem to indicate that an influential family of artisans called the de Polos did indeed live here, and I was shown the house that he was supposedly born in; at the top is a little tower where, according to local legend, the young Marco spoke of his dreams of travelling beyond the distant mountains. Whatever his beginnings, we are sure that Marco Polo was captured by the Genoese in a sea battle that took place in 1298 in these waters.

The Croatian islands were often under attack during the Middle Ages, particularly from pirates and Ottoman ships, which, in the sixteenth century, were manned by Christian captives. There were even stories that the Sultan's harem was full of European women. It was traditions and beliefs such as this that probably led to the emergence of Korcula's second claim to fame: the *moreska* dance (in English, the 'Moorish' dance, subsequently the morris dance) – a traditional sword dance and drama that is still regularly performed today.

Essentially, the *moreska* tells the story of an abducted princess who has been stolen by the Black King from her love, the White King (dressed in red for the dance). As the dance progresses, the armies of the two kings draw swords and 'fight' for the princess. The dance always ends with the restoration of the girl to the White King.

THE PEARL OF THE ADRIATIC

Sailing again along the Croatian coastline, the next stop was Dubrovnik. Dubbed 'the pearl of the Adriatic' by Lord Byron, this is certainly the gem of Dalmatia. Known by its Roman name of Ragusa until the early twentieth century (when it was replaced by Dubrovnik, from the Slavic

word *dubrava* meaning 'oak forest'), the town was founded under similar circumstances to Venice and shares much of its history.

You will find an inhabited walled city, in which there is an east-facing port, which one enters from the west, and it is closed with a chain. It is called Ragusa. In front of the port there is a large, high island called Croma [Lacroma]... Old Raguxi is a great place and from there in a valley nearby there are fresh water mills.

ALVISE DA MOSTO, *PORTOLANO*, 1490

A panorama of Dubrovnik. Its high walls and bastions stand proud above the clear blue sea.

Beginning as a fishing village called Ragusium in the seventh century, it was settled by Romans fleeing the nearby city of Epidaurus (now Cavtat) when it was attacked by the Slavs. During Roman and Byzantine times it flourished as a trading post and during the Fourth Crusade, when Venice consolidated its influence over the coastal and island regions of Byzantium, the

Sponza Palace in Dubrovnik. Built in the sixteenth century, it merges the Gothic and Renaissance styles. It housed some state offices, the mint, the bank, the treasury and the armoury. It was not damaged in the earthquake of 1667, which probably saved the Dubrovnik Republic since affairs of state could continue in spite of heavy destruction.

Venetians helped the Ragusans defend themselves against the advancing Serbs. They also instituted an aristocratic form of government similar to their own, together with a representative of the Doge who was posted here to oversee everything.

In 1358, when Venice lost control in the eastern Adriatic, Ragusa was taken over by the Kingdom of Hungary. This phase lasted less than 50 years, after which the town managed to extricate itself peacefully without falling back into the hands of the Venetians (although this independence came at the price of annual payments to Venice in the form of money and ships). A huge and vibrant community of immigrants, especially Catalans and Florentines, grew up around this centre of trade. One of the most important markets in the early 1400s was for recently discovered cinnabar (used to make vermillion dye). By the middle of the fifteenth century it had a state-funded health service, old people's homes and an orphanage – a reminder, perhaps, that the medieval period was often more 'modern' than we think.

ABOVE Details of Onofrio's Fountain, built by the Neapolitan architect Onofrio della Cava in 1438. In those days most of the cities in Dalmatia, as in Venice, obtained their freshwater supply by collecting rainwater. But the people of Dubrovnik wanted spring water so Onofrio built an aqueduct to this fountain-cum-storage tank.

OPPOSITE The cloister of the Franciscan monastery in Dubrovnik, probably founded by St Francis himself (but in a different location) in the thirteenth century. The pharmacy dates back to 1317, and is one of the oldest in the world.

The golden age came in the sixteenth and seventeenth centuries, before a devastating earthquake flattened the town in 1667, killing half its inhabitants. The rebuilding showed a greater influence of the Slavic style than before, but, like Venice, Ragusa's existence as a city-state was increasingly overshadowed by the might of the surrounding territorial states and in 1806 it was attacked by the Russians and French. Once in the hands of Napoleon's functionaries, they abolished its constitution and, like Venice, the city was passed between the French and Austrians until it eventually became part of Yugoslavia.

Throughout its history the mighty medieval walls surrounding Dubrovnik had made it resistant to attack, but by the second half of the twentieth century these fortifications were thought good only for attracting tourists. However, their defensive function was once again called on when Serbian and Montenegrin forces attacked the city during the 1991 war. Rockets rained down on the red-tiled roofs of the ancient Adriatic port while residents held out for seven months before Croatian reinforcements arrived. A war crime that has rightly put some former Serbian generals in jail, dozens of people died during the shelling and two thirds of the town's architectural heritage was damaged. I asked Katrina, a local artist, what it was like. Her memories were vivid: 'My two kids were little at the time. Everything stopped and we didn't have electricity or water and in the shops everything ran out in a minute…. Whenever we expected bombing, most of the people came into the old town because we believed it was really absurd that anybody would bomb a place protected by UNESCO. The good part is that you become like a family. Not only neighbours, but everyone. We were all asking each other "how are you?", "what's going on?", "can we help each other?". We were like one human being.'

But the harsh memories of the war, the struggle and the efforts to restore the town had not tarnished her sense of belonging: 'You know, I love Dubrovnik, I was born in Dubrovnik and probably I'll live in Dubrovnik forever'. More than a decade after the attack, the Pearl of the Adriatic is recovering its lustre, and the only sign of the bombing is the new tiles on the roofs.

4

∞THE UNKNOWN MEDITERRANEAN

RIGHT A Venetian defence tower at the entrance to the Bay of Kotor (Cattaro).

FAR RIGHT Dawn on the Adriatic coastline.

MONTENEGRO & ALBANIA

We're sailing off the Croatian coast with a fresh cross-wind of 30 knots: with all seven sails unfurled the Black Swan is at her most splendid and we get up to 10.9 knots. The waves lick the deck and salt spatters everywhere, while the roar of the wind covers all other sounds.

Sᴀɪʟɪɴɢ sᴏᴜᴛʜ, we left Croatia behind us, the walls of Dubrovnik running snake-like along the rocky hill face. Greece was some 500 kilometres ahead; in between lay Montenegro and Albania, the 'unknown Mediterranean'. The sea began to make its presence felt and in so doing brought to mind a letter written by Bartolomeo da Mosto on 3 April 1510 when he was in the Bay of Kotor (Bocca di Cattaro), deep inside the Bay of Boka, just beyond the modern-day border between Croatia and Montenegro.

The weather Bartolomeo encountered was very different from our experience. He writes that, due to the dead calm, his galleys had to rely on oars to get to old Ragusa (Dubrovnik) and from there to the bay. The next month, however, everything changed. Leaving the Bay of Kotor he sailed south, day and night, towards Casopo (on the island of Corfu), but gales made things so difficult that he had to tack to windward off the island of Saseno (Sazan, in modern-day Albania). Although he met no other ships on the way, the fact that his fleet had shown itself in front of the Venetian territories in the Adriatic gave heart to their subjects. Sailing in the waters of Budua (Budva) he met two Venetian boats from Candia (Crete) that had abandoned the ships they had been escorting at anchor, since they had been unable to leave the port on account of the weather. Da Mosto accompanied them to Casopo, where they waited for their escort to join them, but he severely reprimanded the Master for leaving them behind, since any small enemy ship, especially pirates, who were plentiful, could have got the better of the two boats had they been separated.

Montenegro got its name from the Venetian sailors who, seeing the dark forested slopes, called them the Black Mountains – *Monte Negro*. The Venetian Republic started taking control of small southern Dalmatian villages in the tenth century, finally managing to create territorial

Aʙᴏᴠᴇ The spinnaker of the *Black Swan*.
Oᴘᴘᴏsɪᴛᴇ Skandebeg's castle at Kruja, where he and the Sultan who had raised him came to blows.

BLACK
SWAN LOG

*I start thinking about all the
strange things that can
happen, for which we now have
scientific explanations. The
Mediterranean is an 'enclosed'
sea, with relatively high salinity,
which increases the buoyancy
for freight ships as they enter it
from the ocean. But when they
go in the opposite direction, out
into the ocean, they have to
watch the Plimsoll line, the
mark indicating the limit for
cargo loads: if they exceed it,
they risk sinking, and once they
pass beyond the Pillars of
Hercules at the Strait of
Gibraltar the lower salinity
increases this risk. Also, when
great air bubbles are released
from the depths of the sea, a
function of rumblings deep
below the earth's crust, a ship
can be sucked down without
warning.*

continuity around the Bay of Kotor in northern Montenegro in the fifteenth century – a dominion that lasted from 1420 until the whole region was swallowed by the Austro-Hungarian Empire in 1797. Other parts of Montenegro constituted the last free monarchy of the Balkans to fall into Ottoman hands, at the end of the fifteenth century. During the sixteenth century, they attained relative autonomy under the Turks, before finally liberating themselves at the end of the seventeenth century after a series of rebellions that culminated in an end to Turkish incursions into Europe. When the Turks started conquering the Balkans in the fifteenth century, however, many Christian Slavs took refuge in Venetian provinces, with the result that, by the late seventeenth century, the Romance language-speaking population of *Albania Veneta* was already a minority compared to the huge Serb and Albanian populations.

Throughout the nineteenth and twentieth centuries, Montenegro lay in the shadow of various Serbian and Yugoslavian nations until, as a result of a referendum on Montenegrin independence in May 2006, the political link between Montenegro and Serbia was finally broken and Montenegro was recognized as one of the world's newest nations.

Scarpello, one of two little islands off the coast of Perast (Perasto), Montenegro, in the Bay of Kotor.

PROTECTION AT SEA

Before coming into harbour at the Bay of Boka, the *Black Swan* set anchor near a tiny island so that I could visit the chapel at the Sanctuary of Our Lady of the Rock. For centuries, Venetian sailors stopped here to leave offerings and to pray for the Holy Mother's protection on their journey. This is the point where the Adriatic waters stopped being unequivocally Venetian and the dangers started to multiply. There are also those who suggest, a little mischievously, that it was here that the commanders and sailors unloaded their lovers before returning home!

According to legend, everything began in 1452, when two fishermen brothers from Perast saw a light shining around an icon of the Blessed Virigin in the waters of a rocky outcrop. Over the years, locals added more and more rocks around the place of the sighting, eventually reclaiming enough ground from the surrounding sea to build a chapel there. In 1628 construction began on a proper church; this was rebuilt in 1720, after the 1666 earthquake. Just behind the main altar is a cavity where the faithful can reach down to touch the rocky outcrop where the icon was found.

Inside the chapel the walls are covered with hundreds of silver plaques that have been left by sailors over the centuries. Some have been very finely crafted by silversmiths; others are clearly the work of the fishermen and mariners themselves. The atmosphere was moving; we walked around in silence, thinking of those who had arrived home safely after leaving a votive offering

ABOVE, LEFT A stone table outside the church, supported by two weary figures.

ABOVE, RIGHT The façade of the sanctuary to Our Lady of Scarpello, designed in the mid-seventeenth century and an important spiritual landmark for Venetian sailors.

BLACK SWAN LOG

The seabed of the Mediterranean is littered with wrecks from Roman times onwards. Leaving the Black Swan for a day, I was taken on a dive to see a wreck in the waters of the Bay of Boka. The Tihany, a typical nineteenth-century Austrian steamship, was 60 metres long and made of iron. It had sailed for many years in the service of the Hungarian-Croatian Company and was seconded to the Austro-Hungarian navy during the First World War. It is intriguing and enticing: a mysterious creature that seems to draw you into its bowels, with no promise that you'll ever emerge again. The ship's timbers have decayed completely, making it possible to inspect the interior, a large cargo hold. The glassless portholes are like deep, round pits surrounded by fronds of seaweed that flicker in and out, as if trying to beckon you into the depths.

here, but also of those who never made it, because of war or the sea itself. And although pirates, bandits and marauding Turks are not common today, I nevertheless felt the urge to make an offering of a small Venetian *gonfalone*.

In spite of the strong winds, we battled our way into the harbour of Kotor, where my ancestors have stayed in good times and bad, leaving their mark on history. In 1545, my namesake, Francesco da Mosto, had his painted portrait reproduced in the frontispiece of the ducal commission that he received as Superintendent in Cattaro (Kotor); he is shown against the landscape of the dark mountains of Montenegro with the Virgin and Child. A copy of this painting hangs at home and it was an odd feeling to see the place with my own eyes, at a distance of nearly half a millennium. Four years later, Valerio da Mosto, Count of Cattaro, issued a coin known as a *mezzo grossetto* that depicted the the patron saint of Kotor on one side and St Mark on the other. Beside the saint's knees was the family coat of arms.

ABOVE Francesco da Mosto kneeling in front of the Virgin and Child.
RIGHT Inside the sanctuary with some of the crew: Lollo, Captain Giulio and Raffa .

THE MADONNA AND THE SEA

I was first told about the Sanctuary of Our Lady of the Rock, which lies off the coast of Montenegro, by my friend Piero Pazzi. Piero is an expert on metalwork and is tireless in his quest to discover and preserve treasures such as this. Before I left Venice he said, philosophically, 'The sea has always been a difficult and dangerous environment, and since ancient times man has entrusted himself to the protection of the gods to defeat the forces of nature that impede and threaten him and his work.'

At the dawn of our own age, female marine divinities were gradually replaced by the figure of the Madonna. To an extent this was due to St Jerome, who, in the fourth century, translated the Bible from Greek and Hebrew into Latin. He claims that the name Mary derives from the Hebrew word *mar* (drop) and *varn* (sea), in Latin *stilla maris* (drop of the sea). Thanks to erroneous transcriptions, *stilla maris* became *stella maris*, star of the sea, an epithet that is still one of the most frequent invocations of the Virgin Mary. One of the most beautiful prayers to the Madonna in this advocation is the *Ave Maris Stella*, composed by the eleventh-

The altar with the icon of
Our Lady and baroque ornamentation.

century monk Hermann the Lame (see below). Hermann was an extraordinary individual. Born horribly handicapped, he was sent to live in a monastery on an island in Lake Constance, founded originally by Charlemagne. Growing up in this religious, learned atmosphere made the most of Hermann's extraordinarily active and vigorous mind. Loved by everyone, this courageous young man learned mathematics, Greek, Latin, Arabic, astronomy and music. He also wrote an entire treatise on astrolabes, in the preface to which he wrote: 'Hermann, the lowest of Christ's poor creatures and of the amateur philosophers, the slowest follower of a donkey, or rather of a snail...has been induced by the prayers of many friends to write this scientific treatise.'

The Church also referred to the Mother of Christ as the *Star of the Sea* because, as St Thomas says, 'just as the sailors are guided to the port by means of the star, so the Christians are guided to heaven by means of Mary'. Thus the Virgin is compared to the Pole Star, the most brilliant and highest of the stars that form Ursa Minor, and the one that acts, as Shakespeare eloquently put it, 'as the star to every wandering bark'.

In the Middle Ages, it was the custom throughout the Mediterranean to throw sacred images into the sea during a storm to placate the forces of nature; they were usually images of the Blessed Virgin and when they were washed up on the shore it was taken as a sign that a church or sanctuary should be built there in honour of the Virgin.

Ave, maris stella, Dei Mater alma, Atque semper Virgo Felix coeli porta.
Sumens illud Ave Gabriélis ore, Funda nos in pace, Mutans Hevae nomen.
Solve vincla reis, Profer lumen caecis, Mala nostra pelle, Bona cuncta posce,
Monstra te esse Matrem, Sumat per te preces, Qui pro nobis natus, Tulit esse tuus,

Virgo singularis, Inter omnes mitis, Nos culpis solutos, Mites fac et castos.
Vitam praesta puram Iter para tutum, Ut vidéntes Jesum, Semper collaetémur
Sit laus Deo Patri, Summo Christo decus Spiritui Sancto, Tribus honor unus.
Amen.

Hail, Star of the sea, Blessed Mother of God and ever a virgin, happy gate of heaven!
Receiving that Ave from Gabriel's lips, confirm us in peace, changing the name of Eva.
Break the sinner's chains, bring light to the blind, drive away our evils, and ask all good things for us.
Show yourself a mother, may He accept our prayers, He who was born for us and chose to be yours.

Incomparable Virgin, meekest of the meek, make us, once absolved of our sins, meek and chaste.
Give us a pure life, and a safe path; that we may see Jesus and rejoice together.
Praise be to God the Father and to the Lord Jesus, and to the Holy Ghost: one honour to all Three.
Amen.

BLACK SWAN LOG

Diving is like entering another world; you don't need a sense of the danger of the depths to feel emotion, you only need to see your companion's eyes to understand it. The only real way of communicating underwater is with hand signals, and there are just a few of these, which are basic and mainly technical: a signal for okay, if everything is going well; one to ask how much air is left in the cylinder; one to say 'let's go up' (or down); and the use of the index finger to point to something. And with the air-supply tube in your mouth it is difficult, if not impossible, to smile, so the only way to express yourself at those depths is with your eyes. The upper world, blithely rushing on its way and burning down the forests that give us our oxygen, simply does not exist down here.

ABOVE Montenegran diver Spaic Bogdan, taking me to look at some underwater relics .

Around the same time, another da Mosto – called Vito – was at work. Also interested in coins, he was, I think, a little less spiritual than my other ancestors. In 1524, the Council of Ten accused him of forging coins and he was arrested. Under torture he revealed that he had an accomplice, Natale Contarini. Both were sentenced to perpetual exile in Famagusta (Cyprus), where they had to present themselves once a week to the captain of the city. The sentence ended with these words: 'If he should be found guilty of forgery in exile, he shall be taken to Venice and between the two columns one of his eyes shall be put out and he shall be sent back into exile. All of his goods shall be sequestered to pay the reward of *LL* 1,500 to anyone who captures him outside his confinement.'

Sanudo, a historian of the day, observed that coining *foreign* currency was actually permitted by the *Serenissima*; so even then the law was perhaps not the same for everyone. Either way, Vito's abilities must have been appreciated, because fifteen years later the Republic appointed him Master of the Gold Fabrics and then chatelain at Cattaro (Kotor), chatelain at Novegradi, a member of the Board of Income, a tax collector *ad officia solita*, and finally *podestà* at Cavarzere, near Venice. In the last years of his life he was a member of the distinguished *Scuola di Santa Maria della Misericordia*!

 STRUGGLES OF ALLEGIANCE AND INDEPENDENCE

It was in Montenegro that the Most Serene Republic was eventually and definitively extinguished. In May 1797, Napoleon conquered Venice and merged it with Italy; later, after the Treaty of Campoformio, he ceded Venice to Austria. It was in the little town of Perast, however, a small city with buildings in the Venetian baroque style, that the *Serenissima* finally folded. Hearing the news that the Doge had surrendered, the people of Perast rejected independence, as they were proud to be Venetian. And even though Venice herself had fallen, and the other colonies were being swallowed up into neighbouring countries, they continued to remain as loyal to the *Serenissima* as they had been for the past 377 years. When, later the same year, the Venetian flag was lowered for the last time and buried beneath the altar of the church, their feelings were clearly expressed in the proclamation written and uttered on the occasion by the Governor, Giuseppe Viscovich:

In this grievous moment, which rends our heart, in this last outpouring of love, of fidelity to the Most Serene Venetian Dominion, to the Standard of the Most Serene Republic, may it be of comfort, O Citizens, that our conduct in former and in recent times makes this fatal act not only more just but virtuous and dutiful for us.

Our children will learn from us, and the story of this day will be known all over Europe, that Perast worthily defended the honour of the Venetian Standard to the very end, honouring it with this solemn act and lowering it bathed in our universal and bitter tears. Let us express our feelings openly, Citizens, and as we seal with our tears the glorious career we have enjoyed under the Most Serene Venetian Government, let us turn to this Banner that represents it and openly vent our grief upon it.

For three hundred and seventy-seven years our possessions, our blood and our lives have always been devoted to You, O St Mark; and we have always been faithful to You and You to us; and with You we have always been illustrious and victorious on the sea.

The town of Perast extends as far as the waterfront would allow, while the dramatic mountainous interior lies a short distance beyond it.

Lions and coats of arms recalling the Venetians who governed Cattaro (Kotor).

With You by our side no one has ever seen us flee; with You by our side no one has ever seen us defeated or fearful!

And if these present times – most unhappy through improvidence, through dissension, through illegal abuses, through vices that offend nature and the rights of peoples – had not taken You from Italy, our possessions, our blood and our life would be devoted to You perpetually, and rather than see You conquered and dishonoured by Your own people, our courage and our faith would be buried beneath You!

But as nothing more can be done for You, may our heart be Your most deeply honoured tomb, and may Your greatest praise be our tears.

GIUSEPPE VISCOVICH, CAPTAIN OF PERAST, AUGUST 1797

Further south, about halfway along the Montenegrin coastline, we stopped over at the port town of Bar to see the ancient remains of Stari Bar. As I walked away from the port to find a taxi to take me beyond the soulless sprawl of the modern town, and looked back, the *Black Swan* looked very odd moored between two huge grey tankers.

Stari Bar, at the foot of Mount Rumija, was settled some 3,000 years ago and since that time has been ruled by Greeks, Romans, Venetians and Ottoman Turks. In the 1870s, Montenegrin rebels, tired of being ruled by foreigners, succeeded in their struggle for independence, but as a result destroyed the town. And what wasn't reduced to rubble then was decimated first by an explosion in a gunpowder warehouse and then by an earthquake in 1979. What is left is an atmospheric ruin, like Pompeii, but dating from the Middle Ages. You can see the old clock

BLACK SWAN LOG

Although the city of Bar has no remarkable architecture or cultural attractions, there is one thing I definitely can't miss: a date with the first person to represent independent Montenegro. Her name is Ivana Knežević, better known as Miss Montenegro 2006. Ivana has lived in Bar all her life, and will shortly be off to university in Belgrade. She is both pretty and intelligent, and proud to represent the new state. Yet this distinction seems to have come about by chance. Last year she was the runner-up in Miss Serbia, when Montenegro was still part of that country. When Montenegro declared its independence, she was called back and proclaimed Miss Montenegro.

ABOVE, LEFT Miss Montenegro looked so much nicer in real life than in a beauty pageant. She has a good head on her shoulders and is keen to progress with her studies.

tower, the Turkish hammam, several churches and even the Venetian fortress. All of this is only just starting to be excavated by archaeologists. I wondered how soon it would be before the town is cordoned off, its treasures placed behind ropes and glass.

 ## A REFUGE FOR PIRATES

For 300 years, until the end of the nineteenth century, pirates from all over the Mediterranean came to settle in Ulcinj, a fortified city perched high above the sea in the south of Montenegro. Piracy was rife in Italy from the Middle Ages onwards, not least because it was both an accepted method of warfare and a way to amass great riches and to ruin your enemy's trade. It was also, for others, a way of gaining a place in paradise, by striking a blow against religious enemies. Local pirate heroes had colourful names such as the Karamindzoja Brothers, Liko Cena and Ali Hodza. Mediterranean corsairs were famously tough, and in this part of the Adriatic it was advisable never to sail at night if you wished to avoid the risk of losing your cargo or being taken prisoner.

There was also a slave market in Ulcinj where prisoners captured from Venetian boats and other galleys were sold. They were mostly slaves from Africa, and included young children, but European nobles who had been captured in battle could also be found. The Tower of the Bal Sié, which has been tidly restored, was the prison where the Spanish writer Miguel Cervantes was detained, and where he was inspired to write the episode of the 'Prisoner' in *Don Quixote*. Cervantes came from a family of modest means. In 1568 he attended college in Madrid, but then fled to Italy after wounding someone, in order to avoid the punishment of having his hand cut off and ten years' exile. As fate would have it, however, he lost his hand anyway, together with the left arm, after being wounded in the Battle of Lepanto. He was known ever afterwards as '*el manco* [one-armed person] *de Lepanto*'. When he had recovered, Cervantes embarked in Naples for Spain with some letters of commendation that were intended to procure him the command of a company. But the galley on which he was travelling was attacked and captured by pirates, and he was held first in Ulcinj and then in Algiers, as a prisoner of the Moors, until finally, after five years, a ransom was paid for him.

A fortress on the hill beyond Ulcinj looms darkly over the thick medieval walls and the narrow stone alleyways of the ancient town, filled with traces of its multifaceted past: Roman columns, decapitated Venetian winged lions, Ottoman crescents and cannon balls.

BLACK SWAN LOG

I have never been to Albania before. I remember that to get from Dubrovnik to Corfu, we almost had to return to Puglia, in Italy, in order to avoid being fired at by the Albanians: this was in the 1980s and Albania was isolated from the rest of the Mediterranean. I was sailing in a friend's boat, Emily VI – and not far into the holiday I realized why there had been five previous Emilies! One evening I did the nightwatch, until four o'clock, when Marino, the owner of the boat, took over and I went to rest. My cousin Sabina, whom I had invited along, had been sick all day. A few hours later I was woken by Marino, speaking quietly but urgently: 'Francesco, Francesco, we're sinking, but don't say anything.' On the floor cooking pots were beginning to float. Still dazed, I went out on deck, where the waves had frothy crests and there was no sign of land. Everyone was bailing out with buckets, while my cousin still lay there, oblivious. I glanced at the lifeboat, imagining my uncle and aunt preparing my crucifixion. What could I do? We checked everything, while the water continued to rise, threatening the electrical equipment. Eventually we found that a cooling pipe had got detached, and instead of running out to sea it was all spilling into the bilge water. The pumps worked hard and gradually the level went down, even though the engine was now at its last gasp.

 OCCUPATION AND SOVEREIGNTY

We travelled on to Albania, which felt even more remote than Montenegro. Albania has had a relatively difficult history, not least because of its position on the Strait of Otranto at the entrance to the Adriatic Sea, which has frequently made it a bridgehead for the conquests of other nations and empires.

Following the pattern of other countries in the region, Albania was occupied by the Illyrians, who were then conquered by the Romans. In the fourth century BC it became part of the Byzantine Empire and thereafter suffered centuries of invasion by Visigoths, Huns, Bulgars and Slavs. In the fifteenth century, the Ottoman Turks took over, cutting Albania off from Western civilization for more than four centuries. In the late nineteenth century, however, the country started reviving its affinities with the West and in 1912 it briefly gained independence, only for the great powers of Europe to assign about half of the Albanian territory and people to neighbouring states a year later. Ruled as a monarchy between the wars, it became a communist state after the Second World War, one which fiercely protected its sovereignty and closely controlled almost every aspect of life. But the collapse of other communist regimes that began in 1989 released new social forces in Albania and although my visit was brief I witnessed many novel democratic processes at work.

At the port of Durres I met Bledi, my Albanian driver, who took me straight to Shkodra (Scutari to the Venetians). Located deep in the heart of Albania, it feels like something from another age. It is hard to imagine that this place was instrumental in the fate of Europe for centuries, being at the frontline of Turkish advances through the Adriatic after they had conquered Greece and much of the western Balkans. But success for the Turks here would have allowed them to push further into the West.

Against the sky, with Shkodra town in the background, looms the imposing castle known by the toponym 'Rozafa'. Perched some 130 metres up, it seems to be clinging to the steep rocks with iron claws. The Buna and Drini rivers flow by on either side and the expanse of Lake Shkodra lies before it. Bronze Age settlements existed here over 4,000 years ago, but the fortress was begun by the Illyrian state in the fourth century BC. Most of what we find today

The evocative fortress at Shkodra (Scutari) in northern Albania. The driver wisely told me, 'Everything begins as a legend, everything continues as in a legend.'

is from the Middle Ages and the most interesting parts of the construction are Venetian, from between the end of the fourteenth century and the late fifteenth. As with many bridges or castles, a legend has evolved about how and when it was built. My driver's version of the Rozafa story is one of the most heartless I've ever heard. He told me that there were three brothers who set about building the castle. They worked all day, but at night the walls fell down. Then an old man advised them that if they wished to ensure the walls stayed up they needed to sacrifice one of their wives. The three brothers couldn't decide which one to sacrifice, so agreed to choose the first wife that brought them lunch the next day. The elder brothers secretly told their wives not to come along that day, and so it was the wife of the youngest, known as Rozafa, who was walled up.

At the main entrance to the castle, where the barbican and the largest defensive tower stand, I looked for remnants of the Venetian presence. The gateway has a pointed arch with a Turkish coat of arms, but emerging to one side of the emblem was the tail of a winged lion carved into the stone. It was here that my ancestors found themselves faced with a great dilemma. The Turkish invasion of Albania began around here and as the Turks' presence in the lower Adriatic gathered momentum, Venice started taking precautions. General Captain Pietro Mocenigo, the captains of the armed trade galleys and other Venetian ships in the area were all told not to return home but to stay in Albania and to prepare their defences, while further reinforcements were sent